REMEMBERING
STEAM

REMEMBERING
STEAM

THE END OF BRITISH RAIL STEAM IN PHOTOGRAPHS

PAUL HURLEY AND PHIL BRAITHWAITE

The
History
Press

First published 2018

Reprinted 2018, 2019

The History Press
The Mill, Brimscombe Port
Stroud, Gloucestershire, GL5 2QG
www.thehistorypress.co.uk

British Library Cataloguing in Publication Data.
A catalogue record for this book is available from the British
Library.

ISBN 978 0 7509 8427 0

Typesetting and origination by The History Press
Printed in China

Above: Standard Class 5 No 4-6-0 No 73129
Winwick Junction, north of Warrington, in 1962. This Standard Class 5 No. 73129 is
the only surviving Class 5 of 30 to be built with Caprotti valve gear and poppet valves,
and it remains at the Midland Railway, Butterly, as a static display. It was built at Derby
Works in August 1956 and was withdrawn from 10C Patricroft on 31 December 1967,
before being taken to Woodham Brothers scrapyard in Barry and rescued from there in
1972 by the Midland Railway Project Group. It was scruffy then, it is not now!

Half Title page: Grange Class 4-6-0 No. 6819 *Highnam Grange*
A sad sight in a Shrewsbury shed in 1962 is this once proud GWR locomotive, *Highnam
Grange*. Built in December 1936 at Swindon Works and scrapped in November 1965
by Cashmore's of Newport.

Frontispiece: 'The Dalesman No. 2 Rail tour' 16 June 1968.
Oliver Cromwell had the leg that ran from the Stansfield Hall/ Copy Pit/ Lostock Hall/
Preston to Carnforth and Skipton leg. The running number was 1Z44.

Title page: A1 4-6-2 No. 60154 *Bon Accord*
Seen at Leeds Neville Hill shed in June 1965, this A1 locomotive was built at Doncaster
Works in September 1949 for British Railways. It was scrapped in October 1965 by
T.W. Ward of Beighton, Sheffield.

Right: Jubilee 4-6-0 No. 45732 *Sanspareil*
An atmospheric photo taken at Preston in 1962, No. 45732 *Sanspareil* awaits the off,
and it looks like the driver is taking a well-deserved cat-nap. The locomotive was built
at Crewe Works in October 1936 and was withdrawn from 9B Stockport Edgeley in
February 1964. It was scrapped at G.W. Butler of Otley on 31 August 1964.

CONTENTS

INTRODUCTION

It is 2018 and that means that it's fifty years since the end of mainline steam on British Railways. Fifty years since that month of August when the last trains hauled by steam locomotives would ever again be seen on the railway lines of Britain. Well, that is what the leaders of British Rail ordered but fortunately it was not to be. Thanks to appeals led by interested parties, including Ian Allan, steam was allowed back on the main lines in 1972. British Rail had already allowed a selection of steam locomotives to be preserved but at the time this was to place them as static exhibits in museums. They then got on with a mass cull of our steam heritage with little thought to just how popular the subject was. It was left to people like Dai Woodham at his scrapyard in Barry Docks to help save over 200 steam locomotives from the cutters torch. Unlike British Rail Management he saw just how popular steam traction was and would become, and without the likes of Mr Woodham there would be a vast shortage of steam traction now.

As it is, new steam locomotives are being built using old plans; the first one is the truly beautiful Peppercorn A1 4-6-2, 60163 *Tornado*, named at York by Prince Charles in January 2009. Trains pulled by it can be seen on the network in all their glory with enthusiasts following its every move. That is not all; around twenty-two brand new steam locomotives are either part-built or on the drawing board, including a member of the 4-6-0 Patriot Class named *The Unknown Warrior* and carrying the number 5551 from one of the unnamed Patriots, a class that had no preservations. Another now lost class the British Rail Standard Class 6, the 4-6-2 Clan Class in the form of 72010 *Hengist*. This was a locomotive on the planned list for the Southern Region but, like others, was never built. It will be now!

But where did it all start? The dawn of the steam age is quite well documented, as it is many hundreds of years since the first experiments into steam power were developed. As for putting the steam-driven engines onto wheels, that is a newer phenomenon – starting as industrial engines and leading up to the Stockton and Darlington Railway in 1825. Then came the Rainhill Trials in 1829 and the following year the Liverpool to Manchester Railway. After this, the railways took off; it was called 'Railway Mania' and was the start of a feeding frenzy for investors with the aim of building a network across the UK. Some worked, and some did not. These were soon sucked into the larger companies, scrapped or joined with others to form more successful business ventures, such as the amalgamation of the Liverpool and Manchester Railway and the Grand Junction Railway.

There was constant development into the twentieth century and in the First World War the railways came under government control working for the war effort in the UK and Europe. Let us remember here that, as well as being fifty years from the last days of steam, it is 100 years in 2018 since the end of the First World War. After the war, it was decided that with around 120 rail companies there were simply too many, so in 1923 the Railways Act of 1921, known as 'The Grouping Act', became law. After this just four large companies known as The Big Four' came into being after incorporating all but a few of the other companies. The LMS (London Midland and Scottish), the GWR (Great Western Railway), the LNER (London and North-Eastern Railway) and the SR (Southern Railway) remained. The biggest of these was the LMS, which became the largest commercial enterprise in the UK and was second only to the Post Office in the number of people that it employed in Britain. It was still all rather unwieldy.

During the Second World War, the railways were again under state control and added greatly to the war effort, but when the war ended they were in a poor state of repair as they had enjoyed little in the way of maintenance. They may have had a big part in winning the war but this came at a great cost to the locomotives and infrastructure. The Labour Party had gained power with thoughts of nationalisation and the railways were in the firing line. In January 1948, the Transport Act of 1947 came into force and the assets of the Big Four were taken into British Railways. Some light railways including the Liverpool Overhead were exempt, but the London Underground was nationalised and came under the London Transport Executive. All other lines became part of the Railway Executive of the British Transport Commission (BTC) under the British Transport Commission Act of 1949. As well as the railways, canals and many other forms of transport fell under the control of the BTC. This altered somewhat five years later when the Conservatives regained control and the power of the BTC was eased by the de-nationalisation and reorganisation of several agencies.

But back to the end of the Second World War, when the government started to look at other methods of power for locomotives. Other European countries had started to rebuild using coal, electric and diesel power. British Rail experimented in the same way but decided to remain with coal as it was plentiful and employed many people in the country. Pre-war locomotives designed by such iconic engineers as William Stanier, Nigel Gresley, Charles Collett, Arthur Peppercorn, John Aspinall and Henry Fowler were upgraded and refurbished by a new generation: George Ivatt, Robert Riddles, Oliver Bulleid and others. There were even some who crossed over themselves at nationalisation, such as Oliver Bulleid, who designed the unsuccessful Leader class of prototype locomotive. The project was scrapped when he took over as CME (Chief Mechanical Engineer) of Irish Railways in 1950.

Between nationalisation and 1960, British Rail built 2,537 steam locomotives, almost 1,000 of which were newly designed Standard locomotives. The idea was for them to be more modern, comfortable to drive and easier to service. We will look at the rather contentious Dr Richard Beeching shortly, but first to consider 'trainspotting' or the word 'enthusiasts' that has succeeded it.

The so-called Baby Boomer generation was made up of many who became trainspotters during the late 1950s and '60s. Mainly schoolboys, with a smattering of schoolgirls, they saw trainspotting as their hobby of choice, standing on stations and tracksides watching, photographing and taking numbers of the myriad classes of locomotives that thundered past. But what about the man who really started it all?

In 1942 the Second World War was ripping Europe apart and 20-year-old Ian Allan was a clerk working for the Southern Railway. He was unfit for the services due to losing a leg at the age of 15 on an outward-bound course with the Officer Training Corps (OTC). He also assisted with the company magazine and in this position he received many requests from enthusiasts for information about the railways. He saw there an opening and after the project was turned down by the management, he published the *ABC of Southern Railway Locomotives* himself. The books gave the numbers, names and details of the engines and classes. He charged a shilling a copy and the first run of 2,000 copies sold out in a few days. His empire had begun and went on to detail all forms of transport and, regarding the railways, the LMS, GWR and LNER areas.

The following year, with colleague Mollie Franklin, who would later become his wife, he set up the Ian Allan Locospotters' Club. By 1951 the club had 150,000 members. The business boomed and the 1956 London Midland Region ABC sold 250,000 copies, which was a record at the time. As other forms of power took over from steam, sales dropped and Ian Allan Publishers Ltd diversified further into all things transport. He purchased two miniature railways and hotels and was very active in the preservation of steam engines. He was also instrumental in the campaign to allow steam back onto the main line in the early 1970s. Ian died in 2015, the day before he would have turned 93.

The nationalisation plan to continue to build and prioritise steam traction was a godsend to rail enthusiasts of all ages. The performance of the BTC through the 1950s was less than satisfactory; continuing to build steam locomotives through to 1960 was a mistake and a waste. But for enthusiasts it was brilliant, so thank you BTC for your help with our hobby, expensive though it was.

Ivatt 2-6-2T No. 41220
Seen at Stockport Edgeley in 1965 is light-duty workhorse, Ivatt-designed
2-6-2T. This particular engine is fitted for push-and-pull work. Built at
Crewe Works in October 1948, withdrawn from 9B Stockport Edgeley in
November 1966 and scrapped at Cashmore's of Great Bridge in June of
the following year.

8F 2-8-0 No. 48476 and Standard 5MT 4-6-0 No. 73069
It is 4 August 1968 and these two coupled locomotives are about to be
joined by a banker in the form of Type 2 Bo Bo Class Diesel number D 7513
as they await their tour of duty. It is on an end of steam special organised
by the Railway Correspondence and Travel Society as the 'End of Steam
Commemorative Rail tour'. More on this train on page 158.

No book covering the end of steam traction or the railways in the 1950s and '60s would be complete without the story of Dr Richard Beeching. Although he was considered a bogeyman in the annals of British Railway, he was not the sole perpetrator of mass closure. Following nationalisation, in 1948 the BTC set up a Branch Lines Committee to investigate branch lines that were losing money. On their recommendation 3,318 miles (5,340km) were ordered to be closed; a few were reprieved after campaigns but most were not. John Betjeman, the famous poet, was instrumental in campaigning for lines to be kept open and this organisation became known as the Railway Development Association. They continued to fight the Beeching cuts that were imposed later. British Rail still lost revenue as well as the fight against increasing road transport and the requirement for government subsidies. By 1955 the income did not even cover the operating costs of British Rail and something drastic had to be done.

Then came the 1955 Modernisation Plan or, to give its full title, the 'Modernisation and Re-Equipment of the British Railways'. The government of the day made a loan to the BTC of up to £250 million (almost £2 billion in 2018), with a rider that it had to be paid back with a proper rate of interest based on the toughest commercial considerations. In retrospect, it was an abject failure. Some parts worked but wish lists such as getting freight back from the roads were naïve in the extreme and led to more wasted income. The electrification of some main lines and the withdrawal of steam in favour of diesel was a rather obvious answer. As an interim measure, capital was expended on new marshalling yards and steam facilities that were soon obsolete. Containerisation increased and became the norm, and many yards were prematurely scrapped. The introduction of untried and hardly tested diesels and electrics contracted out to an assortment of building companies was another mistake. Over the period this saw many breakdowns, with steam traction coming to the rescue.

In 1961, the BTC Chairman was Sir Brian Robertson, earning £10,000 a year; his replacement was Dr Richard Beeching on a salary of £24,000, and the Minister of Transport recruiting him was Mr Ernest Marples. Coincidentally, Marples also had interests in motorway construction, wearing his other hat as former managing director of Marples Ridgeway, a construction firm he still held shares in. No conflict of interest there then! A suitable personage to recruit Dr Beeching who was to shut down large parts of our railway network?

Dr Beeching was, when recruited, the Technical Director of the ICI. At the time, there were mixed feelings about this within British Rail, who would have expected such a post to go to a senior railway officer with knowledge of the job, even though his predecessor, Sir Brian Robertson, was a highly regarded and decorated army general. It was also emphasised that Beeching would be employed for one contract of five years. He was broadly seen in railway circles as a surgeon with the job of robustly cutting back the branches of the network, and so it turned out to be.

The BTC was dissolved and the British Railways Board (BRB) took its place in January 1963 under Dr Beeching. His report, 'The reshaping of British Railways', better known as The Beeching Report, came out in January 1963. It proposed massive closures that would get rid of 5,000 miles of track and 2,363 small stations. This became known as the Beeching Axe. This was short-sighted to many people, as no attempt was made to mothball many of the tracks to see what the future held. They were summarily closed and the tracks ripped up. Soon car parks, houses and shops took the place of stations and rail infrastructure, which made future use impossible. Now congestion on our roads has reached such a stage that many of those abandoned lines could be revenue earning again.

The withdrawal and scrapping of locomotives started towards the end of the 1950s and continued through to the last days of steam in August 1968. Those were the days of the Fifteen-Guinea Special, of enthusiasts thinking that they would never again experience the unique sight and smell of steam locomotives. Those days were just fifty years ago, but that year did not see the end of steam. It is now as popular as ever, albeit in a separate way, and thanks to the demanding work of bands of volunteers it can still be enjoyed and is being enjoyed by many people every year. Railways in general are probably more popular than ever, and as the roads can only get more congested this trend is surely set to continue.

All the photographs in this book were taken by Phil Braithwaite; they depict steam engines and a few period diesels in their natural habitat and the state that they were allowed to enter towards the end.

ACKNOWLEDGEMENTS

With all the photographs taken by Phil, there are not many people to mention. I must mention, however, two excellent websites and the administrators who allowed me to dip into them as part of my research. Firstly, Ian Jenkins of the BRDataBase and Howie Milburn from the RailUK database, both excellent sources of information. Thanks to Ken Issitt, a railway author who kindly submitted a piece, but unfortunately space was against us. Also thanks to Amy Rigg and Jezz Palmer from The History Press for their support and advice; and finally our wives, Rose and Helen, for their patience.

ABOUT THE AUTHORS

Paul Hurley is a writer and member of the Society of Authors. He has contributed to railway and other magazines, written an award-winning novel and twenty-four local history books. He is married to Rose and has two sons and two daughters. He lives in Winsford, Cheshire.

Phil Braithwaite has been a railway photographer since the late 1950s in both the UK and South Africa, photographing the last of steam traction in that country. He is the owner of a Thomas Green & Son 1924 steam roller and van. Phil lives with his wife Helen in Barnton, Cheshire.

Black Five 4-6-0 No. 44832
A locomotive hard at work with a smoky fire in the firebox and a relatively short goods train lays down a smokescreen as it heads south at Moore Lane Bridge in 1965. Built in Crewe Works and into service in August 1944, the last allocation being 5B Crewe South from where it was withdrawn in September 1967 and taken to T.W. Ward of Killamarsh for scrapping in December of that year.

5MT 4-6-0 No. 44937
An engine at speed here as Black Five 44937 heads north at Moore Lane near Warrington in 1965. The Stanier locomotive was built at Horwich Works in November 1946. The last shed was 68A Carlisle Kingmoor, from where it was withdrawn on 31 May 1967 and scrapped at J. McWilliams of Shettleston in November of that year.

Black Five 4-6-0 No. 44803
An action shot of a hard-working Black Five at it climbs the bank out of Warrington southbound, in 1964. Built at Derby Works in 1944 and withdrawn from 26A Newton Heath in June 1968 to be scrapped three months later at Drapers, Neptune Street Goods Yard, Hull.

Moore Lane Bridge
Moore, south of Warrington, on a busy summer Saturday. No numbers here but what does it matter with such an excellent 1964 photograph of a busy scene. A BR Standard class 4-6-0 heads a passenger train whilst an unidentified steam engine waits with its mixed goods on a two-road storage siding. This line is mainly used for freight trains awaiting to slot in between the busy Chester and North Wales trains. Travelling in the same direction on the main line is a period diesel railcar.

9F 2-10-0 unknown number
The engine number is not known on this action shot of a dirty 9F heading towards Warrington southbound at Winwick in 1965.

Manor Class 4-6-0 No. 7802 *Bradley Manor*

One of Charles Collett's light engines designed for secondary lines is seen here with a passenger train near Oxley Motive Power Depot (MPD) in 1963. Built at Swindon Works for the GWR in 1938. Its last shed was 84G Shrewsbury, from where it was withdrawn in November 1965. One of nine of these fine engines to be preserved 7802 *Bradley Manor* was fortunate in being sent to Woodham Brothers scrapyard in July 1966. It spent fourteen years there until it was rescued by the Erlestoke Manor Fund based at the Severn Valley Railway. The original plan was to use it for parts for the *Erlestoke Manor*. Fortunately, there was a change of heart and *Bradley Manor* was beautifully restored and returned to work on the preserved lines and the main line by 1993. At the time of writing it is back on the rails.

Two 5MT's Nos 44776 and 44854

A peep into Leeds Holbeck shed in 1963. Black Five's 44776 and 44854 were built at Crewe Works in 1947 and 1944 respectively. No. 44776 was withdrawn from 8F Springs Branch in May 1967 and scrapped at Cashmore's five months later. 44854 was withdrawn from 55E Normanton and scrapped at T.W. Ward of Killamarsh in December.

5MT 4-6-0 No. 45081

A Black Five here with a self-weighing tender heads north through Warrington Bank Quay station in 1964. The self-weighing tender is quite an unusual feature. Basically, it was a Standard type tender with a sort of hi-ab contraption on the rear to weigh the coal going into the tender. Mainly fitted to Black Fives but also other classes. This engine was built at the Vulcan Foundry in March 1935 and withdrawn from 12A Carlisle Upperby in October 1965, being scrapped at Campbells of Airdrie in March 1966.

A3 Class 4-6-2 No. 4472 (60103) *Flying Scotsman*

Probably the most famous locomotive in the world photographed when steam could still be found on the main lines. It was already in preservation on excursion 1X44 as it heads towards Chester at Moore Lane, south of Warrington, on 4 June 1966.

Here is an example of the interest that there was in main line steam even before the mass culling of steam engines. The engine was built at Doncaster Works in February 1923, having been designed by Nigel Gresley. Its first BR shed was 36A Doncaster and it was withdrawn in January 1963 from 34A Kings Cross. In 1924, the engine was displayed at the British Empire Exhibition and it was here that her fame began. With the addition of a special tender that had a corridor through to the train enabling the crew to change without stopping, it was the first engine to pull a train non-stop from London to Edinburgh. In 1934, it achieved 100mph on a test run.

When withdrawn it was purchased by Alan Pegler, who was a member of the British Rail Board under Richard Beeching. The board had refused permission in 1962 for this already famous engine to be photographed next

to a new Deltic on the anniversary of its record-breaking run. Beeching promptly sacked Pegler for his impertinence in saving the engine against the will of the board, who wanted to look forwards and not backwards. This is another example of the apparent short-sightedness of a man who seemed to consistently take no account of strong public feelings regarding his plans.

It was given a complete overhaul in 1969 prior to a tour of the USA, where it was stranded for a while due to Alan Pegler going into bankruptcy. William McAlpine put together a rescue plan and the engine toured Australia before returning to continue with its duties on Britain's railways, but with several new owners and many ups and downs.

In 2004, the National Railway Museum started a campaign to save what had become a national treasure and the oldest steam locomotive still on the main line. With grants from the National Heritage Memorial Fund and the Heritage Lottery Fund, not to mention massive support from the public, the engine is once again in tip-top condition. At the time of writing, this national treasure is still hard at work and is booked to run specials on the main line for the foreseeable future.

Britannia Class 4-6-2 No. 70042 *Lord Roberts*

This powerful Britannia heads an excursion southbound at Moore near Warrington in 1966. The Riddles-designed locomotive was built at Crewe Works in April 1953. Its last shed was 12A Carlisle Kingmoor, from where it was withdrawn on 13 May 1967 and scrapped five months later at J. McWilliams of Shettleston.

Deltic Class D9001

It's May 1963 and in a yard comprising mainly steam traction Deltic D9001 heads away from Doncaster station with a rake of seven maroon BR coaches. Still five years to go before the end of mainline steam but diesel is starting to get a foothold, and in other parts of the network it will be joined by electric traction. Things were changing and changing fast. The locomotive was built by EE/VF (English Electric/Vulcan Foundry) and was introduced in February 1961. It received its TOPS number (Total Operations Processing System) 55001 in February 1974 and was named *St Paddy*. It was withdrawn in January 1980 and cut up at Doncaster Works the following month.

8F 2-8-0 No. 48735
A smoky 8F can be seen heading north at Winwick Junction north of Warrington in 1966 with a mixed goods train. The Stanier 8F was built at Darlington Works, going into service in November 1945. Its last shed was 8E Northwich, from where it was withdrawn on 14 October 1967 and later scrapped.

BR Standard Class 4-6-0, 4MT No. 75020
Seabirds and their calls compete with the steady throb of the BR Standard 4MT working in its home territory as it approaches Barmouth in North Wales. It has just crossed the Barmouth Bridge in July 1965 with a short train. Built at Swindon Works on 30 November 1953 and designed at Brighton Works by R.A. Riddles. This 1965 shot shows the engine with the 89A Oswestry shed plate. It would soon be transferred to 11A Carnforth, from where it was withdrawn on 31 August 1968. It went from there to Campbells of Airdrie to be scrapped three months later.

8F 2-8-0 No. 48628 GWR Manor and Class 4-6-0 No. 7824 *Iford Manor*
At Oxley now, a suburb of Wolverhampton, as 8F 48628 and its goods train are about to cross paths with Great Western Manor Class 7824 *Iford Manor*. The year is 1963 and the 8F is about to enter its own yard at Oxley as the *Iford Manor* passes with a special. What is about to occur in trainspotting parlance is a 'black out', when two trains pass and it hides the number of one of them. No. 48628 was built at Brighton Works during 1943, going into service in May of that year, again with the LMS, not the WD. In September 1966 it was withdrawn from Oxley MPD, being scrapped in February 1967 at Cashmore's Great Bridge. 7824 was built at Swindon Works and going into service in December 1951. It was withdrawn in November 1964 and also scrapped at Cashmore's of Great Bridge.

8F 2-8-0 No. 48103
The fireman casually leans out of the cab window as his light engine heads north of Warrington in 1966. The engine was built at Crewe Works, going into service during February 1939. The last shed was 16C Derby, from where it was withdrawn in October 1966 and scrapped the following February.

GWR Pannier Tank
The number is not known here but the photo is pure steam days. The short goods train passes the Wellington signal box in 1966. Your photographer and co-author Phil Braithwaite spent many hours in this signal box, enjoying brews and chats with the signalman, so there are a few more photographs from this location thanks to the signalman's excellent tea.

9F 2-10-0 No. 92234
The same location as the previous shot, but this time a sturdy 9F passes Wellington signal box with a mixed goods in 1966. The Riddles locomotive was built at Crewe Works in August 1958. This powerful engine with a life expectancy of at least thirty years was withdrawn from 8H Birkenhead Mollington Street in December 1966 and scrapped at Campbell's of Airdrie three months later at the ripe old age of eight!

Diesel Class 47XX No. D1711
A very attractive photograph of a diesel of the period. The guard's van seen on the left is at the rear of the train just featured, 9F 92234, at Wellington signal box in 1966. The diesel D1711 was built by Brush and went into service in January 1964. It was later given the TOPS number 47122 and was withdrawn in September 1987, being cut up at M.C. Processors of Glasgow in October 1989.

Patriot Class 4-6-0 No. 45512 'Bunsen'
This rebuilt Patriot Class engine is seen heading south at Moore Lane, Warrington in 1962. The locomotive was built at Crewe Works in 1932 and withdrawn from 12A Carlisle Kingmoor on 27 March 1965 then scrapped at Motherwell Machinery and Scrap, Inslow Works, Motherwell. It was one of the last rebuilt Patriots to be withdrawn and none were saved. A new build is believed to be on the cards though.

Britannia Class 4-6-2 70014 *Iron Duke*

The driver leans in a position that he will have leant in many times, this time in the powerful Britannia Class locomotive and its fitted freight. The train is passing through Preston station in 1966. This locomotive class was designed by Robert Riddles; he was Director of Transportation Equipment during the Second World War and had been responsible for the design of the successful WD Austerity 2-8-0 and the WD 2-10-0. After the war, he applied to be Chief Mechanical Engineer of the LMS but the job went to George Ivatt. In 1947, the Railway Executive came into being and he was appointed as a member of the board with responsibility for mechanical and electrical engineering. Effectively, with his two assistants, he performed the duties of the old Chief Mechanical Engineer.

In this capacity he oversaw the design of the BR Standard Classes. One of these was the Britannia Class and from 1951 to 1954, fifty-five members of the class were built, of which *Iron Duke* was one. He used his experience from the days before nationalisation to look back at the designs of Oliver Bulleid and his Light Pacifics. The result was a locomotive capable of heavy freight and fast passenger work, designed at Derby Works and built at Crewe Works. The first engine was named after a suggestion by acclaimed railway photographer Bishop Eric Treacy, *Britannia*. The locomotives were scattered around the country and the names reflected this. Great Britons were mainly used; in Scotland the names of Scottish Firths were used, and the Western Region used the names of Star Class locomotives.

Iron Duke was built in June 1951 and allocated to 32A Norwich Thorpe. Its last shed was 68A Carlisle Kingmoor, from where it was withdrawn in December 1967 and scrapped at T.W. Ward of Killamarsh on 12 March 1968.

Castle Class 4-6-0 No. 5081 *Lockheed Hudson*
Built on 31 May 1939 at Swindon Works as *Penrice Castle*, seen here heading a return south freight from Hereford in May 1963. One of a large class of 171 locomotives, it had a name change in January 1941. In common with several of its classmates, it was renamed in tribute to the RAF aircraft of the period, in this case one of the RAF bombers, the Lockheed Hudson. The locomotive was designed by Charles Collett, Chief Mechanical Engineer of the GWR. Its last allocation was 88B Cardiff East Dock, from where it was withdrawn on 31 October 1963 for scrapping at R.S. Hayes/Birds, Tremains Yard, Bridgend, It was broken up on 30 June 1964.

Jubilee Class 4-6-0
Number and name not known but well worth a look as a Jubilee Class 4-6-0 is seen at Winwick Junction north of Warrington in 1966.

8F 2-8-0 No. 48135

In 1965 an engine with its train of ICI tanks heads north at Moore Lane near Warrington. It passes the old bricked-up tunnel as a trainspotter notes down the number from the side of the track. The Stanier engine was built at Crewe Works during May of 1941 and unusually went to the LMS rather than the WD. In 1950, it could be found at 13D Northwich working the ICI ash trains from Buxton, a normal use for this class of engine. It returned to 8E Northwich on 25 March 1957 from where it was withdrawn in September 1965 and scrapped at Cashmore's of Great Bridge three months later.

8F 2-8-0 No. 48391

It's 1964 as 8F 48391 heads a freight south out of Warrington Bank Quay station. The locomotive was built at Horwich Works and went into service in April 1945. It was withdrawn from Newton Heath on 18 December 1965 and scrapped at Cashmore's of Great Bridge three months later.

Hughes Fowler Crab 2-6-0 No. 42771

Standing forlorn and withdrawn at 20A Leeds Holbeck in 1963 is this Hughes Fowler Crab. It was built at Crewe Works in July 1927 and withdrawn from this shed on 23 November 1963, being scrapped at Crewe Works on 31 December of that year. Known colloquially as Crabs, this class of engine was designed by George Hughes, who was the CME of the LMS between 1923 and 1925. The class was built between 1926 and 1932, the work continued by Hughes' successor Henry Fowler. The name Crab was used partly because the unique inclined cylinders represented a crab's claws, but also because of the feeling on the footplate that the engine was 'scuttling' along the track. They were also called 'Horwich Moguls' as the first batch was built at the Horwich Locomotive Works.

Fowler 0-6-0 No. 44345

A look now at a locomotive with delusions of grandeur. It is travelling through Warrington on the main line, single engine with 'The Royal Scot' chalked on the front, the year is 1964. The Fowler engine was built by Kerr-Stuart, going into service during January 1927. It was scrapped at Loom Albert at Spondon in November 1964, having been withdrawn from 13C Heaton Mersey.

Royal Scot Class 4-6-0 No. 46128 *The Lovat Scouts*
Heading south out of Warrington Bank Quay station in 1965 is 46128 rebuilt
Royal Scot, *The Lovat Scouts*. It was built at the North British Locomotive
Company in Glasgow in 1927 and withdrawn from 68A Carlisle Kingmoor on
1 January 1965 before being cut up at Motherwell Machinery and Scrap of
Inslow Works, Wishaw, two months later.

Unnamed Britannia Class 4-6-2
The photograph was chosen for its ethereal beauty. This Brit is on the platform at Crewe with a night parcels train. It is 1966 and the engine has already lost its nameplates as the driver in his cab – illuminated by the open firebox – chats to a member of staff on the platform. A typical evening scene at Crewe station before the end of steam. Many enthusiasts with flasks and sandwiches have sat on a cold platform waiting for just such a sight.

B1 Class 4-6-0 No. 61008 *Kudu'*
Seen on York MPD is the B1 61008 and the year is 1962. It was designed by Thompson and built at Darlington Works, going into service on 13 May 1944 at Darlington. Transferred to the Scottish Region in March 1963, it was withdrawn from 66E Carstairs in December 1966 and scrapped two months later at J. McWilliams of Shettleston.

Jubilee Class 4-6-0 No. 45726
Vindictive
Heading a fitted freight at Arpley Warrington low level line towards Stockport during 1963. *Vindictive* was built at Crewe Works in 1936 and withdrawn from 8B Warrington Dallam on 20 March 1965. It was cut up at T.W. Ward of Beighton, Sheffield, three months later.

5MT 4-6-0 No. 44896
A very attractive ex-works engine takes on water at Newton Heath MPD in 1964. Standard Black Five 44896 was built at Crewe Works in September 1945. It was withdrawn twenty-two years to the day later at 20A Leeds Holbeck and scrapped at Cashmore's of Great Bridge on 31 May 1968.

Hall Class 4-6-0 No. 7906 *Fron Hall*

Seen on Shrewsbury MPD during 1964 in company with an unnamed diesel hydraulic. *Fron Hall* was designed by Hawksworth and built at Swindon Works in December 1949. Its last allocation was 81F Oxford, from where it was withdrawn in March 1965 and scrapped at Swindon Works two months later.

Manor Class 4-6-0 No. 7818 *Granville Manor* and No. 6853 *Morehampton Grange*

Two for the price of one now as we take a peep into Shrewsbury shed MPD in 1963. The first one is No. 7818, built for the GWR at Swindon Works in January 1939 and withdrawn from 48E Tyseley in January 1965, being scrapped at Cashmore's Great Bridge three months later. No. 6853 was also built for the GWR at Swindon Works in November 1937 and withdrawn from 84E Tyseley in October 1965, being cut up at Cohens of Kettering, five months later.

Manor Class 4-6-0 No. 7818 *Granville Manor*
At Shrewsbury in 1964 as a smart 7818 *Granville Manor* turns sedately around on the turntable to return from whence it came.

Coronation Pacific Class 4-6-2 No. 46228 *Duchess of Rutland*
One of the most beautiful classes of engine, No. 46228 is turned on the Shrewsbury Motive Power Depot turntable in 1962. It was cut up on 31 December 1964, having been designed by William Stanier and built at Crewe Works on 30 June 1938 as one of the original streamlined engines. It was de-streamlined in 1947. Its last shed was 5A Crewe North, from where it was withdrawn on 30 September 1964 and cut up at Cashmore's of Great Bridge three months later.

Coronation Class 4-6-2 No. 46228 *Duchess of Rutland*
Another look at *Duchess of Rutland* on the turntable at Shrewsbury.

Black Five 4-6-0 No. 45483
64A Edinburgh St Margaret's shed in 1965 and we have a clean, possibly ex-works Black Five standing amongst the fire bricks. The locomotive has been fitted with a tablet-catching apparatus and was built at Derby Works in 1943. It was withdrawn from St Margaret's in December 1966 and scrapped at Motherwell Machinery and Scrap, Inslow Works, Wishaw during November 1967.

V2 Class 2-6-2 No. 60844
A dark and gloomy day in Edinburgh at 64A St Margaret's MPD in 1965.
A Gresley V2 engine stands over the pits in steam and ready to go. The
engine was built at Darlington Works in 1939 and allocated to this depot.
It was withdrawn from 62B Dundee Tay Bridge in November 1965 and
scrapped at the Motherwell Machinery and Scrap of Inslow Works, Wishaw,
the following month.

0-4-0 Saddle Tank *Asbestos*

Oh, if only the crystal ball people could have got it right they would have seen the problems that the product of this works would have in store. Not British Railways but well worth a mention with such an important period photograph. The ominous name of this saddle tank is simply *Asbestos* and it was built by Hawthorne Leslie in 1909 with the works No. 2789. It is seen shunting in the sidings of the Turner & Newall Works on Trafford Park in 1962. It was a massive works that met its demise in 2001 and by this time the legal claims were mounting up. The engine, however, came out of it all quite well – it is preserved at the Chasewater Railway in Staffordshire.

A busy scene at Dallam MPD, Warrington, in 1961
A look at a typical steam shed in the early 1960s, Dallam MPD in
Warrington. The two engines on view are Fowler Patriots 45549, unnamed,
and 45503 *The Royal Leicestershire Regiment*. Both are Fowler rebuilds of
LNWR Claughton engines – No. 45549 in 1934 and No. 45503 in 1932.
Both were built and scrapped by Crewe Works. No. 45549 was withdrawn
from Dallam in 1961 and No. 45503 from 12B Carlisle Upperby in 1962. The
Royal Scot nearest the camera is 46102, *Black Watch*, a Fowler design with
Stanier rebuild. It was built at the North British Locomotive Works, Glasgow,
in 1927 and withdrawn from 67A Corkerhill in December 1962, then cut up
at J. McWilliams of Shettleston. An elusive engine for enthusiasts!

Peppercorn Class 7 Pacific 4-6-2 No. 60530 *Sayajirao*

The detritus of a busy workshop lies around as an enthusiast by fair or innocently foul means has gained access. He is faced with what must be quite a good 'cop', the 4-6-2 locomotive *Sayajirao* standing with the front end on jacks as it awaits further attention. The date is 1964 and this snapshot in time takes place in a corner of Darlington Works. It is receiving light casual maintenance and would leave the works in October of that year.

On 17 December 1953, the engine was involved in a serious crash at Longniddry in Scotland. It was hauling a special Christmas-parcels train from Edinburgh to Kings Cross when it struck an object on the line that had fallen from a goods train. The fireman was killed and the driver seriously injured when the engine was thrown over the station platform and down an embankment, landing with its wheels in the air. It was taken to Doncaster Works and took just forty-three days to repair.

The locomotive was built in these works and released in March 1948 for delivery to its first allocation, which was 34A Kings Cross. It had the LNER number 530 which the following year became BR 60530, although the name had been with it from the beginning. Its last shed was Dundee Tay Bridge, from where it was withdrawn in November 1966 and cut up at Motherwell Machinery and Scrap, Inslow Works, Wishaw four months later. Like all but one of the class that was named in honour of the designer A.H. Peppercorn, *Sayajirao* was named after a racehorse.

LNER B16 4-6-0 No. 61435
Stopped in the yard at Doncaster MPD in 1963 is B16 61435, the last one of the class in service. Designed by Raven and updated by Gresley, it was built in November 1922 at Darlington Works. Its last shed was 53A Hull Dairycoates, from where it was withdrawn on 31 July 1964 and scrapped four months later at Draper's of Hull.

Hughes-Fowler Crab 2-6-0 No. 42940 alongside 5MT No. 44836
Stockport Edgeley MPD now in 1964 and a Hughes-Fowler Crab stands in steam next to a 5MT. The Crab was built at Crewe Works in December 1932 and its last shed was this one from where it was withdrawn on 25 September 1965 and cut up at T.W. Ward of Killamarsh, three months later. The Stanier Black Five was also built at Crewe Works with this as the last shed; it was also cut up by T.W. Ward, but at the Beighton scrapyard.

Manor Class 4-6-0 No. 7812 *Erlestoke Manor*

Pure Great Western here as *Erlestoke Manor* is seen on the turntable at Shrewsbury in 1962. This Collett engine was built for the GWR at Swindon Works in January 1939. Its last main line shed was this one, 84G Shrewsbury, from where it was withdrawn in November 1965. 7812 *Earlestoke Manor* was one of the four GWR-built Manors to be preserved. It was one of the engines sent to the Woodham Brothers scrapyard, Barry, where it quietly decomposed until it was rescued by the Erlestoke Manor Fund in 1974. After an overhaul, it entered service on the Severn Valley Railway in 1979. It is currently owned by the Earlestoke Manor Fund and is operational on the SVR.

Manor Class 4-6-0 No. 7812 *Erlestoke Manor*

Another look at the preserved locomotive *Erlestoke Manor*, now over the pits at Shrewsbury MPD in 1963.

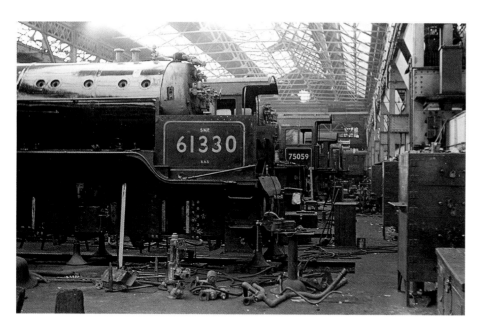

The erecting shop at Darlington Works, 1964
A look here into a typical railway workshop, as locomotives are lined up partway through various stages of maintenance. The nearest to the camera is Thompson-designed LNER B1 4-6-0 No. 61330 built at the North British Locomotive Works in Glasgow and entering service in June 1948 at 35A New England. It was in Darlington Works for a total of forty-three days from 7 September 1964. The last shed was 62A Thornton Junction, from where it was withdrawn on 19 November 1966 and scrapped the following month at Motherwell Machinery and Scrap at Wishaw. The next engine is 75059 Riddles-designed Standard Class 4. Built at Swindon Works and entering service in April 1957, it was withdrawn from 10A Carnforth in July 1967 and scrapped at Campbells of Airdrie five months later.

5MT 4-6-0 No. 45070
A nice crisp shot of a Black Five on the Shrewsbury turntable in 1963 as the driver takes the opportunity to let off a little steam. The locomotive was built at Crewe Works, going into service in May 1934. It had many allocations, ending up at 8B Warrington Dallam from where it was withdrawn in May 1967 and scrapped two months later at Cohens of Kettering.

B1 4-6-0 No. 61224 and Q6 0-8-0 No. 63348
Inside the roundhouse at Leeds Neville Hill MPD on 14 September 1963, where we have a pleasant view of the quiet interior of this typical roundhouse. Q6 63348 is standing on the turntable. This Raven-designed locomotive was built at Darlington Works in March 1913 and its last shed was this one, from where it was withdrawn in June 1964 and scrapped two months later at W. Willoughby, Choppington. Nearest the camera No. 61224 was built at the North British Locomotive Company, Glasgow, in October 1947, the last shed being 56A Wakefield from where it was withdrawn on 31 July 1966 and scrapped two months later at Hesslewoods of Attercliffe.

Black Five 4-6-0 No. 45313 with diesel shunter No. D2391

At Dallam MPD in Warrington during 1962 is this Black Five, built at Armstrong Whitworth in February 1937. It was withdrawn from 10A Wigan Springs Branch on 28 February 1965 and scrapped at the Central Wagon Company, Ince Wigan, the following month. The 0-6-0 diesel-mechanical shunter was built at Doncaster Works in 1961 and withdrawn from 8F Springs Branch, Wigan, in 1970 to be scrapped at G. Cohen of Kettering, in November 1971 after a period in storage.

Two GWR Pannier Tanks and 8F 2-8-0 48665 at Croes Newydd shed

A very atmospheric shed scene here at a completely run-down 6C Croes
Newydd shed in 1967. The two pannier tanks seen here have shed plate
6C painted on. At the time, there were three saddle tanks allocated to
Croes Newydd – numbers 1628, 3709 and 9630. The 8F 48665 was built at
Brighton Works in March 1944 and was withdrawn at the end of steam in
August 1968 from 10F Rose Grove and was scrapped in the same month.
At the time of the photograph it was probably also based at Croes Newydd,
which closed on 5 June 1967, so the dereliction was probably understandable.

Standard Class 3 2-6-2T No. 82031
Barmouth station, looking down on Standard Class 3 2-6-2T No. 82031 in 1964. This Riddles-designed engine was built at Swindon and allocated to 88C Barry in December 1954. It is seen here with a short local train. It was withdrawn from 10C Patricroft in December 1966 and scrapped at Cashmore's of Newport, in June the following year.

WD 2-8-0 No. 90386

Darlington Works is seen here at an open day in September 1964 and what better star of the show than an Immaculate ex-works WD 2-8-0 No. 90386. It was one of a class of 733 locomotives based on the Stanier LMS 8F as reworked by R.A. Riddles to prioritise low cost due to the ongoing war, and the need for powerful locomotives at the expense of good looks if necessary. This one was built at the North British Locomotive Company in Glasgow, going into service in January 1944 and attached to the War Department with the number 78592. It was purchased from the department by the fledgling British Railway in November 1949 and given the number 90386. In 1950,

it could be found allocated to 66B Motherwell and its last shed was 62C Dunfermline Upper, from where it was withdrawn in April 1967 and cut up at Motherwell Machinery and Scrap, Inslow Works, Wishaw five months later. The saddle tank peeping from the shed is 0-6-0ST No. 68011 another R.A. Riddles-designed ex-War Department locomotive. It was built in 1944 by the Hunslet Engineering Company and delivered to the War Department in May of that year. Sold to the LNER in 1946 with the number 8011 and then transferred to British Rail on nationalisation and given the number 68011, it was withdrawn from Darlington in May 1965 and cut up at Cohens of Cargo Fleet five months later.

Standard Class 4MT, 4-6-0 No. 75033

It is early 1967 at 6C Croes Newydd shed, Wrexham, and we see one of R.A. Riddles Standard Class of locomotives, designed at Brighton Works, simmering away amongst the rubbish of a dying shed. The shed would be closed that year. The locomotive was built at Swindon in July 1953. It was withdrawn from 11A Carnforth in December 1967 and cut up at T.W. Ward of Killamarsh, in June 1968.

Thompson B1 Class 4-6-0 No. 61135

A great swathe of Doncaster station and yard is spread out before the camera as Thompson B1 61135 leaves the platform with a short passenger train in early 1963. The train consists of a delightful selection of carriages and the locomotive would not last much longer. It was built during March 1947 at the North British Locomotive Company, Glasgow. The last shed was 36A Doncaster, from where it was withdrawn on 22 September 1963 and there scrapped the following month.

A1 Class LNER Pacific 4-6-2 No. 60128, *Bongrace*
Up to Scotland now and into the shed at Edinburgh, St Margaret's. The date is circa 1961 as A1 Pacific 60128 simmers gently in line outside the shed building. The locomotive, designed by Peppercorn, was built for British Railways in May 1949. The last shed was 36A Doncaster, from where it was withdrawn in January 1965 and scrapped the following month at Drapers, Neptune Street Goods Yard, Hull.

Jubilee Class 4-6-0 No. 45580 *Burma* with Black Five No. 45150
On Warrington Dallam MPD in 1962 with Jubilee, 45580 *Burma*. The engine was built at the North British Locomotive Company in Glasgow in October 1934. Its last shed was 26A Newton Heath, from where it was withdrawn on 12 December 1964. In April 1965 it was cut up at T.W. Ward, Beighton, Sheffield. The Black Five 45150 was built at Armstrong Whitworth in June 1935 and its last shed was 9E Trafford Park, from where it was withdrawn in March 1968 and scrapped at Drapers, Neptune Street Goods Yard, Hull, three months later.

V2 2-6-2 No. 60905
On Doncaster MPD in May 1963 and we find a Gresley-designed V2 60905 flashed up and ready to go. The locomotive was built at Darlington Works and went into service on 10 April 1940. Its last shed was 36A Doncaster, from where it was withdrawn in September 1963 and scrapped at Doncaster Works the following month.

0-6-0 Tank No. 47383
Back to Dallam MPD in 1963, where a little Jinty is trapped between two larger engines. The Jinty was built at the Vulcan Foundry in October 1926 and was probably luckier than its two big friends for it was preserved. It was withdrawn from 16G Westhouses on 7 October 1967. It is currently a static exhibit in the Engine House on the Severn Valley Railway but will eventually be overhauled and returned to the metals.

5MT 4-6-0 No. 44761 and Britannia 4-6-2 No. 70052
Firth of Tay
Newton Heath MPD in 1962 and two engines are in view. The first, Stanier Black Five 44761, was one of the last of the class built at Crewe Works in October 1947. It lasted almost to the end, being withdrawn from 24C Lostock Hall on 30 April 1964 and cut up at Cohens, Kettering in September 1968. The Riddles-designed Britannia engine 70052 *Firth of Tay* was built at Crewe Works during August 1954 and lasted to 1 April 1967, when it was withdrawn from 68A Carlisle Kingmoor and scrapped at Campbells of Airdrie in October of that year. We cannot leave it there, however, as *Firth of Tay* was the offending locomotive in the Settle rail crash on 21 January 1960. The locomotive was descending Ais Gill summit with the Glasgow St Enoch to London St Pancras express in severe blizzard conditions. One of the connecting rods came loose, seriously damaging the opposite rail as the engine went along. A goods train hauled by a Black Five was travelling in the opposite direction and was derailed, causing the goods train to collide with the side of the express ripping out the first three carriages and scoring the remainder. Five people were killed and eight more injured. One of the dead was a 23-year-old man on the way to join the RAF while another, an elderly man, was with his wife on their way to retire in Devon.

Jubilee Class 4-6-0 No. 45705 *Seahorse*
Complete with yellow stripe but no nameplates, No. 45705 *Seahorse* is seen on Trafford Park MPD in 1964. It was built at Crewe Works in May 1936 and withdrawn from Newton Heath in November 1965 to be scrapped at Cashmore's of Great Bridge in February 1966. More on this locomotive later in the book.

LMS Coronation class 4-6-2 *46245 City of London*

This beautiful locomotive is seen in all its shining glory hauling an Ian Allan Railtour IX91 on 1 September 1964. The route was from London Paddington to Crewe where a tour of the works was enjoyed and then returned to Paddington. The locomotive was thanked for this duty by being withdrawn and scrapped almost immediately.

The class, known as the Coronation Class or Princess Coronation Class, was designed by William Stanier for the London Midland and Scottish Railway. The first of the class was 46220 Coronation built in 1937. The class consisted of thirty-eight locomotives, designed and built as a larger and more improved version of the Princess Royal Class that preceded it.

The original plan was to build more Princess Royal class engines when it became obvious that more would be needed, especially with plans being drawn up to start a non-stop through train from London to Glasgow. Stanier was persuaded by Tom Coleman, Chief Draughtsman and Technical Assistant at Derby works, to go back to the drawing board and design a brand-new class of locomotives. The result was the Coronation Class – more powerful and easier to maintain than its predecessor, the Princess Royals. Stanier was however contracted to fulfil an assignment in India, leaving Mr Coleman to complete the plans for the new locomotive that would be the most powerful in the LMS.

The locomotive was almost ready to be built when it was discovered that the London and North-Eastern Railway had introduced the A4 Class, it was streamlined, making it a design popular with enthusiasts and the public alike.

The railway companies were very mindful of other railway companies and, like the Ocean Liners competing for the Blue Riband at that time, they were in competition to have the fastest main line trains. Accordingly, the decision was made to streamline the new locomotives. The result was beautiful; there were some problems with smoke not being deflected away from the drivers cab, but it was beautiful all the same. The first five were built at Crewe Works in 1937 and painted in Caledonian Railway blue with silver horizontal lines that matched the coaches of the Coronation Scot trains that they were specifically built to haul. During the press run that year 6220 *Coronation*, driven by Driver T.J. Clarke, Fireman C. Lewis, Robert Riddles as the engineer and Inspector S. Miller, broke the previous record held by the LNER of 113mph by doing 114mph on the Madeley Bank north of Crewe. Catastrophe nearly struck however as the train approached Crewe station, those on the footplate were so elated that they did not notice at first that they were still doing 110mph. The train took the stations reverse curves that had a speed limit of 20mph at 57mph. Fortunately the only damage inflicted was an uncomfortable ride for the passengers and some broken crockery. A truce was declared though between the companies because of the scare. This lasted until the following year when the LNER engine 4468 Mallard hit 126mph while 'trialling a new brake system'.

46245 *City of London* was built in June 1943 and in 1948 could be found at 1B Camden shed. Its last allocation was 5A Crewe from where it was withdrawn in September 1964 and scrapped at Cashmore's of Great Bridge three months later.

5MT 4-6-0 No. 45344
Another wet day in 1963 as Black Five 45344 with a passenger train is stopped at Shrewsbury station platform with plenty of leaking steam. The engine was built by Armstrong Whitworth, going into service in April 1937. It was withdrawn in August 1966 and cut up at Cashmore's of Great Bridge the following March.

A3 Class 4-6-2 No. 60080 *Dick Turpin*
A rather scruffy Gresley-designed A3 locomotive awaits departure at Edinburgh Waverley in 1962. It was built for the LNER at the North British Locomotive Company, Glasgow, going into service on 3 November 1924. On 23 October 1925, it spent four days at Gateshead Works where it received a light service and was named *Dick Turpin*. In 1942 it was rebuilt from an A1 and in 1961 the German-type smoke deflectors were fitted. It was withdrawn from 52A Gateshead in October 1964 and scrapped at Drapers Neptune Street Goods Yard, Hull, on 31 December 1964.

Jubilee Class 4-6-0 No. 45626
Seychelles
Leeds City station, on 3 October 1964 and Jubilee Class 45626 pulls into the station bearing the head code lights for a passenger train, breakdown train and newspaper train, watched by a large crowd of enthusiasts. Also in the photograph is a Stanier tank No. 42189 and the Peak Class diesel D190. *Seychelles* was built at Crewe Works in November 1930 and withdrawn from 20A Leeds Holbeck in November 1965, being cut up at T.W. Ward, Killamarsh, two months later. The Fairburn Tank engine was built at Derby Works in November 1947 and withdrawn from 20D Normanton for cutting up at Cashmore's of Great Bridge in May 1968. D190 was built by BR Derby and introduced in January 1963. It later received the TOPS number 46053 and was withdrawn and cut up at BREL, Derby, in July 1981.

4MT 2-6-0 43140
An atmospheric shot here of a 4MT 'Flying Pig' sat at the platform at Manchester Victoria as the driver chats to another railwayman in 1962. The engine was designed by Ivatt and built at Doncaster Works, entering service on 8 August 1951 at 64E Polmont. Its last shed was Normanton, from where it was withdrawn during June 1967 and scrapped at Drapers, Neptune Street Goods Yard five months later.

Black Five 4-6-0 No. 45156 *Ayrshire Yeomanry*
It's August 1968, the last month of regular steam on British Railways, and
one of only four named Stanier Black Fives stands in a bay at Manchester
Exchange. *Ayrshire Yeomanry* was built at Armstrong Whitworth in July
1935. It was withdrawn in August 1968 from 24B Rose Grove after working
the last of the specials, and cut up at T.W. Ward, Beighton, Sheffield, four
months later. There were originally five named Black Fives, the fifth being
45155 *The Queen's Edinburgh* but this one had the name removed in 1944.
Some preserved Black Fives have been named, but only 45154 *Lanarkshire
Yeomanry*, 45156 *Ayrshire Yeomanry*, 45157 *The Glasgow Highlander* and
45158 *Glasgow Yeomanry* were originally named and retained their names
almost until withdrawal. None were preserved.

Jubilee Class 4-6-0 No. 45563 *Australia*
At Warrington Bank Quay station on shunting duties in 1964 is 45563 *Australia*. It should be said that using this engine as a shunter is like using a Rolls-Royce as a builder's van. It was built in August 1934 at the North British Locomotive Works in Glasgow and withdrawn from Warrington Dallam in November 1965. It was cut up at Cashmore's of Great Bridge, in April 1966.

Coronation Class 4-6-2 No. 46238 *City of Carlisle*
Preston station in 1962 and a beautiful and powerful Coronation Class engine stands at the platform being admired by a grown-up enthusiast and presumably his young son. The Stanier locomotive was built at Crewe Works and entered service in September 1939; a look at the lower front end tells us that it was once streamlined but is now what is known as a 'Semi' for 'Semi-Streamlined'. It was withdrawn in October 1964 and scrapped at Arnott Young of Troon two months later.

Fowler 2-6-4 Tank No. 42394

Station pilot at Leeds City station in 1963 and standing at the platform side is a Fowler 2-6-4 tank engine, No. 42394. The engine was built at Derby Works in June 1933 and withdrawn from 55A Holbeck on 4 January 1966, one of the last two of the class to be withdrawn and cut up at Drapers, Neptune Street Goods Yard, four months later. No members of this large class were preserved; however, there are plans for a new one to be built in the coming years by the LMS Patriot Class on completion of the new *Unknown Warrior*.

Standard Class 2 2-6-0 No. 78037
It's 1964 and this 10-year-old engine enters Preston station with a short trip freight consisting of two wagons and a guard's van. Not the most lucrative job but no doubt it will be added to later to give the guard more of a job. The Riddles-designed engine was built at Darlington Works in November 1954. Its last shed was 24C Lostock Hall, from where it was withdrawn in May 1967 and scrapped at Motherwell Machinery and Scrap of Inslow Works, Wishaw, six months later.

Fowler 0-6-0 No. 44294
Complete with its yellow stripe to bar it from going south of Crewe,
No. 44294 is seen on station pilot duties at Warrington Bank Quay station in
1965. The 4F was designed by Fowler and built at Derby Works in 1927. It
was withdrawn from Warrington Dallam in November 1965 and scrapped at
Cashmore's of Great Bridge in July 1966.

A1 4-6-2 No. 60145 *Saint Mungo*
During an open day at Darlington Workshops on 3 October 1964 we can see Peppercorn A1 *St Mungo* in for an overhaul. The locomotive was built during March 1949 at Darlington Works for BR. Its last shed was 50A York North, from where it was withdrawn in June 1966 and cut up at Drapers, Neptune Street Goods Yard two months later. None of the class was preserved but as previously mentioned a new one has been built, 60163 *Tornado*. St Mungo was a Scottish saint.

A4 4-6-2 No. 60007 *Sir Nigel Gresley*

The location is Carlisle station and in the distance can be seen, looking very smart, Coronation Class 4-6-2 No. 46256 *Sir William A. Stanier FRS*. Both are running various legs of 'The Scottish Lowlander Tour', on 24 September 1964. A4 No. 60009 *Union of South Africa* also provided some assistance on the route. Phil was on the tour from Crewe and back to Warrington. *Sir Nigel* and *Union of South Africa* have been preserved, *Sir William A. Stanier FRS* was shockingly cut up at Cashmore's of Great Bridge in December 1964. So being in such cosmetically excellent condition can probably be put down to overnight work by a group of enthusiasts. This iconic engine had only three more months in service.

Mid-summer and a train in the distance

How it used to be and how we followed trains. It is around 1962 in the Warrington area and we see two typical trainspotters/enthusiasts watching the steam train in the distance travelling along an embankment. This shot will bring back memories for anyone around at the time. It is obviously mid-summer and we have a racing bike, a camera and holdall, bike clips and flat cap. Those days did seem more innocent and carefree.

Hughes Fowler Crab 2-6-0 No. 42792
One of the ubiquitous Hughes Fowler Crabs is seen at Dallam shed about to be turned on the turntable in 1963. This is shortly before withdrawal, as shown by its appalling condition. The Hughes-derived Fowler engine was built at Crewe Works in October 1927 and its last shed was 39A Gorton, from where it was withdrawn on 26 October 1963 to be scrapped at Rigleys of Bulwell Forest in January 1964. The enthusiasts here are perhaps in a precarious place!

Standard 4 2-6-0 No. 76020 and Q6 0-8-0 63393

Darlington Works on 3 October 1964 and we see two locomotives being viewed by a group of mature enthusiasts. No. 76020 was built at Doncaster Works during December 1952. Its last shed was 6A Chester, from where it was withdrawn on 30 April 1966 and scrapped at Birds of Long Marston three months later. The engine behind it is Q6 0-8-0 63393 that was built at Darlington Works during October 1918, having been designed by Vincent Lichfield Raven, CME of the North-Eastern Railway (NER) from 1910 to 1922. The engine's last shed was 54B Tyne Dock, from where it was withdrawn on 30 June 1964 and cut up at Darlington Works four months later.

01 Class 2-8-0 No. 63687

The past hauls the future here as No. 63687 arrives at Doncaster, with two baby Deltics (D5900s) in tow, in May 1963. The engine was designed by John George Robinson, CME of the GCR, and built by Robert Stephenson and Hawthorn Ltd in 1924. As an 04 Class, it was later rebuilt under Thompson as an 01 Class with an upgraded boiler, new cylinders and Walschaerts valve gear. It was withdrawn on 16 October 1963 from 31B March and scrapped in January 1964 at Doncaster Works.

K4 Class 2-6-0 No. 3442 (61994) *The Great Marquess*

Seen at Leeds City station on 3 October 1964, this beautiful preserved
locomotive is leading an Ian Allan excursion, 1Z10, 'The Darlington
Marquess Rail Tour'. It took the first section of the tour from Leeds to
Harrogate with four coaches and was joined at Harrogate by 4472 (60103)
which had brought the main tour portion, on the ECML, from Kings
Cross. The tour then proceeded to Darlington Bank Top. This photo shows
that even when steam could be found on the main line, engines were
being preserved and used on enthusiast specials. The enthusiasts around
the engine are making the most of this treat to see a locomotive in this
condition, when all around are dirty unkempt engines.

The Gresley engine was built in June 1938 at Darlington Works specifically
for working the West Highland Line from Glasgow to Mallaig, which has
steep gradients and many tight curves. This is mainly where it spent its

Scottish and British Rail days. The last shed was Dunfermline, from where
it was withdrawn in December 1961 and purchased from British Rail by the
Scottish Lord David Lindesay-Bethune the 15th Earl of Lindsay, Viscount
Garnock. From 1968 it was stored away due to the ban on steam, then in
1972 it was moved to the Severn Valley Railway where Viscount Garnock
had been chairman. In 1980 it was given a full overhaul and rebuild that was
completed in 1989, when it returned to hauling specials. Viscount Garnock
was there for the first outing and in fact travelled on the footplate: not a well
man at the time, he sadly died a short while later. The engine passed to his
son Jamie but soon its maintenance required spending money so he sold it
to his neighbour John Cameron, on the condition that it returned to work in
Scotland. John Cameron already owned *Union of South Africa.* He kept to
the promise and *The Great Marquess* worked in Scotland for a while as well
as spending time hauling specials on English metals.

Jubilee Class 4-6-0 45705 *Seahorse*

Details about *Seahorse* have already appeared in this book, but an excellent photo such as this cannot be missed. Enthusiasts are all over the track at Cheadle Heath station in September 1965 as *Seahorse* waits to take over from *Flying Scotsman* on the LCGB High Peak Railtour. The original was scrapped at Cashmore's of Great Bridge in 1966 but a beautiful 3½-inch gauge model of it can be seen running on the Pembrey Miniature Railway in Carmarthenshire. After a recent full service, it is now a perfect miniature of this engine.

Riddles 4F 2-6-0 No. 43139

A rather more powerful engine than the usual station pilot, but at Carlisle station that is what was on offer on 13 February 1965. Also known as a 'Flying Pig' or 'Mucky Duck', this Riddles engine is being admired by a group of enthusiasts. It was built at Doncaster Works in July 1951 and its last shed was 68A Carlisle Kingmoor, from where it was withdrawn in September 1967 and cut up at Motherwell Machinery and Scrap of Inslow Works, Wishaw in February 1968.

Castle Class 4-6-0 No. 7029 *Clun Castle*

Towards the end of steam on the GWR there were several specials and *Clun Castle* hauled the last official steam train out of Paddington on 11 June 1965. This photograph was taken on 4 September 1965 when *Clun Castle* has been especially rostered to be the last steam-hauled Summer Saturday special on the Honeybourne Line. It was the IM39, 12.30 p.m. from Penzance to Wolverhampton. The engine spent the next two years working the 'Last day of Steam' specials, of which there were many due to demand. The actual last day of mainline steam on the Southern Division of British Rail was Sunday, 9 July 1967. Collett-designed *Clun Castle* was built at Swindon Works in May 1950 and its last shed was 35B Gloucester, Horton Road, from where it was withdrawn on 31 December 1965. It was bought for its scrap value of £2,400 in 1966 by railway preservation pioneer Patrick Whitehouse. It then went to the Clun Castle Ltd for preservation, still in good condition, and continued hauling specials until the official end of steam on British Rail. Then again from 1972 until the need for a major overhaul until 1985, when it once again resumed work on the main line. At the time of writing it is coming to the end of another overhaul.

Standard Class 5, 4-6-0 No. 73067
Another look at Shrewsbury station on a wet 25 September 1965 as a British
Rail Standard Class 5 drifts in light engine to the delight of the enthusiasts.
Built at Crewe Works and going into service during October 1954, it was
withdrawn from 9H Patricroft in March 1968 and scrapped at Cashmore's of
Great Bridge three months later.

A2/3 4-6-2 No. 60522 *Straight Deal*

In the erecting shops at Darlington Works on 3 October 1964. Apart from the class leader, which was named after the designer Edward Thompson, all were named after racehorses. There were just fifteen in the class, as the next fifteen were redesigned by Thompson's replacement, Arthur Peppercorn, and became standard A2 class. No. 60522 was built at Doncaster in 1947 just before nationalisation, withdrawn in June 1965 and cut up at Motherwell Machinery and Scrap, Inslow Works, Wishaw.

Jubilee Class 4-6-0 No. 45646 *Napier*
Jubilee *Napier* passes Warrington South signal box from Chester in 1960. The locomotive was built at Crewe Works and went into service on 14 December 1934. Its last shed was 25G Farnley Junction, from where it was withdrawn on 28 December 1963 and scrapped at Darlington Works three months later.

NB J36 0-6-0 No. 65267
Now we have a venerable engine that worked on the railways of Britain for seventy-four years, four months and one day. It is seen here complete with battered snowplough in Bathgate MPD, Edinburgh, in 1964. It was built for the North British Railway in July 1892 at the Cowlairs Works. It was finally withdrawn from 64F Bathgate in November 1966 and scrapped at Arnot Young of Old Kilpatrick in April 1967. Rather sad really.

8F 2-8-0 48258
Hauling freight northbound towards Winwick Junction north of Warrington in 1963. An ex-works 8F No. 48258, the locomotive was built at the North British Locomotive Works in Glasgow during October 1941 but not, as with a lot of the class built then, for the War Department. Instead this one went straight to the LMS. The first allocation on amalgamation was 5B Crewe South but then loaned to 9G (later 8E) Northwich for a brief time. The last shed was 8A Edge Hill, from where it was withdrawn on 26 October 1967. It was scrapped at J. Buttigiegs of Newport in January 1968.

Castle Class 4-6-0 No. 5092 *Tresco Abbey*
Here *Tresco Abbey* is heading south on a Cardiff–Manchester express near Hereford in May 1963. Churchward/Collett engine 5092 *Tresco Abbey* was built at Swindon Works for the GWR in April 1938. Well, that's not totally correct, it was a rebuild of Star Class 4072 *Tresco Abbey* built in 1923 and rebuilt as 5092 *Tresco Abbey*. Its last shed was 88L Cardiff East Dock from where it was withdrawn on 31 July 1963 and scrapped at Cashmore's of Newport, on 31 October 1964.

Opposite: Hughes-Fowler Crab 2-6-0 No. 42793
It is 1965 and a set of new electric units destined for the Birkenhead/Liverpool railway is seen at Moore Lane towards Chester, circa 1964. The steam engine hauling the next generation of railway traction is Hughes-Fowler Crab 42793. The locomotive was built at Horwich Works in October 1927. Its last shed was 9B Stockport Edgeley in 1964, from where it was withdrawn and scrapped at Wards of Broughton Lane, Sheffield, in March 1965.

Jubilee Class 4-6-0 No. 45643 *Rodney*
At Leeds Holbeck MPD in 1963 and we see this relatively clean Stanier
Jubilee *Rodney*. It was built in December 1934 at Crewe Works and
withdrawn from this MPD on 31 January 1966 then scrapped at Clayton &
Davy, Dunston-on-Tyne.

70013 *Oliver Cromwell*
A look at the locomotive that was to star during the last days of steam. It is seen here in shed with enthusiasts admiring it. The last British Rail steam locomotive to have a routine heavy overhaul at Crewe Works, it ran from 3 October 1966. It was intended from then to be preserved and it was prepared for the end of steam specials. If it was to fail during these duties it could have been ruthlessly withdrawn. Plenty more on this engine later.

5MT 4-6-0 No. 44853
An ex-works Black Five at Crewe station in 1963, No. 44853 shunts the parcels trains. It was built at Crewe Works, going into service during November 1944. Its first and last British Rail shed was 20A Leeds Holbeck, from where it was withdrawn in June 1967 and scrapped at Cohens of Kettering five months later.

Jubilee No. 4-6-0 No. 45600 *Bermuda*
Leaving Warrington Bank Quay station in 1964, this Stanier designed engine was built at the North British Locomotive Company and went into service on 2 February 1935. It was withdrawn from 9D Newton Heath on 18 February 1965 and scrapped at Cashmore's of Great Bridge four months later.

Jubilee Class 4-6-0 No. 45556 *Nova Scotia*

No. 45556 heads south towards Warrington in 1966. The Stanier Jubilee was built at Crewe Works in June 1934 – one of the first in the class built as a development of the Patriot Class but with a taper boiler. The last shed was 5A Crewe North, from where it was withdrawn in September 1964 and cut up four months later at Birds of Morriston.

Royal Scot Class 4-6-0 No. 46115 *Scots Guardsman*

Scots Guardsman was one of the two Royal Scot engines that would be preserved, but here we look at the locomotive as it heads the evening parcels train northbound near Moore in late 1965. Built at the North British Locomotive Company, Glasgow in 1927 and withdrawn from 68A Carlisle Kingmoor on 1 January 1966. This Fowler-designed engine was rebuilt by Stanier during LMS days. Fitted with a taper boiler, double chimney and new cylinders.

Q6 0-8-0 No. 63370

Now this locomotive looks quite old and it is, built at Darlington Works in April 1917 and seen here in Leeds Neville Hill MPD on 14 September 1963. It was designed by Vincent Raven, later Sir Vincent Raven, CME of the North-Eastern Railway from 1910 to 1922. This locomotive was withdrawn from this MPD in June 1964 and scrapped at Darlington Works the following month.

Jubilee Class 4-6-0, No. 45732 *Sanspareil*

Seen in the confines of Preston station, No. 45732 awaits the off with a goods train in 1963. The class was introduced in 1934 as an upgraded version of the Patriot Class, designed by William Stanier with his trademark taper boiler. This engine was built on 29 October 1936 and withdrawn from 9B Stockport Edgeley on 29 February 1964. Six months later it was cut up by G.W. Butler, Otley.

A1 4-6-2 No. 60128 *Bongrace* and V2 2-6-2
Already featured earlier in the book but it's worth another look at this
Peppercorn-designed A1 on Doncaster MPD in May 1963 behind an
unidentified V2.

Black Five 4-6-0 No. 45312
Open day at Corkerhill MPD in 1964, with a view of a Black Five locomotive in an ex-works condition. It looks even better when you notice the other engines in that line are not quite as well turned-out. This Stanier engine is an example of the superb class that it belongs to. It was built during February 1937 at Armstrong Whitworth for the LMS and taken into British Rail on nationalisation. The reason for its condition is that it had just enjoyed the ministrations of Cowlairs Works, from where it was released in April 1964. It was withdrawn from 9K Bolton in June 1968 and was cut up at Cohens of Kettering in February 1969.

8F 2-8-0 No. 48451

This light engine, waiting for the signal at Winwick Quay yard, north of Warrington, in 1963 is one of the true workhorses of the days when steam ruled the rails. No. 48451 was built at Swindon Works in September 1944 for the LMS, not the War Department like some of its classmates. This massive class of Stanier locomotives, which if I remember rightly were nicknamed 'Consuls', were the backbone of heavy freight duties. This one was withdrawn from 10F Rose Grove on 4 May 1968.

Fowler 0-6-0 4F No. 44237

One of the ubiquitous Fowler 0-6-0 engines runs tender-first on a trip freight through Warrington Bank Quay station to the low-level sidings, north of the station in 1962. The engine was built at Derby Works, going into service in March 1926. It was withdrawn from 8B Warrington Dallam in March 1963 and scrapped at C.C. Crump Ltd of Connah's Quay on 30 April 1964.

Jubilee Class 4-6-0 No. 45695 *Minotaur*

Left and below: This badly damaged engine was involved in a crash at Broadheath near Altrincham on 18 January 1964 near No. 3 signal box on the Arpley line. A signalman wanted to take a goods train off the main line for the Liverpool to York mail to pass through. He made a mistake with the signal and sent the rear guard's van and rear wagons of the goods train back on to the main line. No. 45695 hauling the mail train ran into them at around 40mph, causing it to crash into a bridge and sustain the damage that we see here. The engine was taken to Altrincham where it remained for two months before it was cut up at J.S. Parker, Broadheath, Altrincham. 45695 *Minotaur* is a member of the Jubilee Class, built by Crewe Works in 1936. Its last shed was 25G Farnley Junction. Fortunately, and perhaps amazingly, no one was seriously injured in the crash.

Britannia Pacific 4-6-2 No. 70022 *Tornado*

A Britannia Class Pacific in rather good condition is seen northbound at Moore in 1964. No. 70022 has a parcel train; the Riddles-designed engine was built at Crewe Works in August 1951. Its last shed was 12A Carlisle Kingmoor, from where it was withdrawn on 23 December 1967 and three months later cut up at T.W. Ward of Inverkeithing. The bricked-up tunnel that can be seen on the left of the photograph was the Acton Grange railway tunnel. It was 108 yards long and on the line from Warrington Bank Quay to Moore. It was opened in 1888 and closed in 1893 when the line was deviated.

Collet 3 MT 0-6-0 No. 2253

This locomotive is seen shunting its train at Ross-on-Wye in 1963. The engine was built at Swindon Works during March 1930 having been designed by Charles Benjamin Collett CME of the GWR from 1922 to 1941. Its last allocation was 85A Worcester, from where it was withdrawn on 31 March 1965 and scrapped at Swindon Works two months later.

9F 2-10-0 No. 92233

Here in 1964 a relatively new Riddles 9F 92233 fitted with double chimney is leaving the old LNWR Arpley line at Warrington low level. It is heading towards the 12 Arches yards, just across the Mersey. The Riddles-designed engine was built at Crewe Works during August 1958 and allocated to 86G Pontypool Road. It was withdrawn from 8C Speke junction on 29 February 1968 at the grand old age of nine years and five months. T.W. Ward of Beighton cut it up in August 1968.

Standard Class 4 No. 75014

Standard 75014 heads out of Shrewsbury past Sutton Bridge signal box for the Cambrian coast in 1963 with a passenger train. The infrastructure of the old railways can be seen here, from the water stand pipe with its small brazier to fight off the frost to the myriad of lines going off in all directions. The locomotive was built during November 1951, and it was withdrawn from 84G Shrewsbury on 31 December 1966. It doesn't end here though; it was one of the lucky engines sent for scrap at Barry scrapyard, where it resided until 1981 when rescue arrived in the form of a syndicate affiliated to the North Yorkshire Moors Railway and by 1994 it was back in steam. The then owner sold it to the Dartmouth Steam Railway in 2002 who named it *Braveheart*. After more work, the locomotive was ready for business in 2016 and is now a frequent visitor to the main lines of Britain with a boiler certificate that runs until 2026.

B1 4-6-0 No. 61255
This Thompson-designed B1 was built just before
nationalisation in November 1947 at the North British
Engineering Company, Glasgow. It is seen here on the
Doncaster turntable in May 1963 as it provides the power
to enable it to turn. It gives the crewman a chance to
have a quiet cigarette. It was withdrawn from 53A Hull
Dairycoates on 24 June 1967 and scrapped two months
later at Garnham, Harris & Elton, Chesterfield.

Black Five 4-6-0 No. 44756
Smoke drifts from the chimney of this rather dirty
Black Five seen here at Newton Heath MPD in 1963.
The engine was built in June 1946 at Crewe Works,
incorporating a steel firebox, Caprotti valve gear, Skefko
roller bearings and a double chimney. It was withdrawn
from 13E Brunswick on 30 September 1964 and scrapped
at W.E. Smith of Ecclesfield, on 28 February 1965.

9F 2-10-0 No. 92157
Preparing for a hard day's work by filling the tender of No. 92157 with coal under the coaling plant at Edge Hill MPD Liverpool in 1966. Designed by R.A. Riddles and only built at Crewe Works in November 1957, this engine looks in remarkably good condition for a young engine about to be withdrawn. And so it was, in August 1967 at the ripe old age of under ten years, it was withdrawn from 6C Birkenhead. It was then scrapped at J. Buttigiegs of Newport in January 1968.

K1, 2-6-0 62041
Seen here at Darlington Bank Top, banking an Ian Allan special to Darlington works. The engine pulling the train is 2-6-0, 61994 the preserved engine *The Great Marquess* on 3 October 1964. This is the reason that the driver, fireman and even the guard are looking not back, but forward into the station as *The Great Marquess* leaves the station. 62041, is pushing the train assisting its Thompson designed class member to pull the heavy train. The locomotive was designed by Edward Thompson and his assistant Arthur Peppercorn who became CME on Thompson's retirement and continued with the design of the K1. It was based on the earlier K4 that was introduced in 1937 and most of the class was built at The North British Locomotive Company in Glasgow between 1949 and 1951 for British Rail. The class consisted in total of seventy-six that included seventy class K1, Class K1/1 and five Class 4s. Just the first six were named including the preserved *Great Marquess*. 62041 was built in 1949 and scrapped at Drapers, Neptune Street Good Yard, Hull in September 1967.

Standard Class 2 2-6-0 No. 78002
A busy engine on station pilot duties
at Preston in 1964 is Standard Class 2
No. 78002. As it sits between two carriages,
a member of the crew adjusts the running
lights. The locomotive was designed, as
were most of the Standard engines, by R.A.
Riddles at Derby and introduced in 1952.
This engine was built at Darlington Works
in December 1952. It was withdrawn from
24C Lostock Hall in June 1966 and cut up
at the Central Wagon Co. of Ince, Wigan,
four months later.

**Standard Class locos 4-6-2T's Nos 80000
and 80115**
Up to Corkerhill MPD, Glasgow now to
see two Standard Class 4-6-2 tank engines
parked in amongst the firebricks in 1964.
A youth dressed in typical 1960s clothing
runs away from the camera, possibly
because he has heard of a far more
interesting locomotive in another part of the
works – or he may have been spotted by a
member of staff! 80000 was built at Derby
Works in September 1952 and allocated
to 67C Ayr. The last shed was this one,
from where it was withdrawn in December
1966 and scrapped four months later at
Shipbreaking Industries, Faslane. No. 80115
was built at Doncaster in December 1954
and allocated to 66A Polmadie, from where
it was withdrawn in October 1964 and
scrapped at Motherwell Machinery and
Scrap of Wishaw in February 1965.

Crostie Boilered 9F 2-10-0 No. 92025
This not very successful experimental Riddles 9F heads east at Skelton
Junction in 1965. It had been built in 1955 and fitted with a Crosti Boiler
and pre-heater. This had been sealed off in 1959 for orthodox working.
Built as a sub class of ten experimental Riddles locomotives at Crewe Works,
No. 92025 ended its working life at 8C Speke Junction. From there it was
taken to Campbell's of Airdrie for cutting up in April 1968.

Britannia Class 4-6-2 No. 70005, *John Milton*
A crisp, but very smoky, photograph taken as Riddles Britannia Class engine
John Milton heads north at Moore Lane, Warrington in 1967. The nine-coach
train is no trouble for this powerful locomotive. Built at Crewe Works in 1951,
it was withdrawn from 12A Carlisle Kingmoor on 10 October 1964. It was
scrapped in January 1968 at Campbells of Airdrie.

WC Class 4-6-2 No. 34104 *Bere Alston*

Seen at Weymouth in 1965 is a scruffy version of a once proud rebuilt and Bulleid-designed West Country Class/Battle of Britain 4-6-2 in the form of *Bere Alston*, minus its nameplates. It is surrounded by the detritus of an MPD, a common site at the time. The locomotive was built at Eastleigh Works, going into service in April 1950 as an air-cooled 'Spam Can', then it was the last of the class to be rebuilt in May 1961. The last shed was 71A Eastleigh, from where it was withdrawn in June 1967 and cut up at Cashmore's of Newport.

Bournemouth Station
A period look now at Bournemouth station in 1965, a happy holiday
destination throughout the years. And it continues to serve that purpose
today, albeit somewhat modernised. Here an unknown steam engine is
preparing to shunt the carriages.

View of the yards at Weymouth MPD in 1965

What a scene of devastation here: rebuilt Merchant Navy Class 4-6-2 35022, *Holland America Line* nearest the camera was withdrawn in May 1966 from 70G Weymouth Radipole. This rebuilt Bulleid engine was built at Eastleigh Works during October 1948. On withdrawal, it was taken to Barry scrapyard in South Wales where it remained rotting until 1983, when it was rescued by the Southern Steam Trust. It is now stored at Crewe Diesel TMD awaiting restoration.

West Country/Battle of Britain Class un-rebuilt 4-6-2 34102 *Lapford*, nicknamed 'Spam Cans' was still in steam here but the future was not so bright. Built at Eastleigh Works and into service in March 1950, the last shed was 70D Eastleigh, from where it was withdrawn in July 1967. Despite appeals it was eventually scrapped on 30 September 1968 by Cashmore's of Newport.

MN 4-6-2 No. 35022 *Holland America Line*

We have already looked at this locomotive and in this shot it hasn't moved but waits to do so, as it is parked amongst the oil drums at Weymouth in 1965. So, let us look at the diesel that shares the yard – D7079. It was built by Beyer Peacock and entered service in December 1963. It was withdrawn in October 1971 and cut up at Swindon Works in August 1972. The steam engine still exists, however.

Coronation Class 4-6-2 46256 *Sir William A. Stanier FRS*

Continuing our look at the Coronation Class with this photo of one of the youngest members, 46256 *Sir William A. Stanier FRS*. In 1938 the second batch of locomotives was built but they were painted in crimson lake with guilt horizontal lining. In 1939 the new *Duchess of Hamilton* swapped nameplates with 4-6220 *Coronation* for a tour of the USA. It was accompanied by a train of new articulated coaches matching the colour of the engine and was to visit the World's Fair. So, for a while there was a red 6220 *Coronation* with a large spotlight and bell on the front in the USA and a Blue 6229 *Duchess of Hamilton* in the UK! This wasn't the first train trip to the USA, in 1893 the London and North-West Railway sent the locomotive *Queen Empress* and two carriages to the World's Fair at Chicago. Then in 1933 the LMS locomotive *Royal Scot* was taken for a tour of the USA, followed by a five-month display at the Century of Progress exposition in Chicago.

But back to the Coronation Class: later in 1938 the second batch was built but Stanier decided to build them without streamlining due to the extra weight and accessibility. A fourth batch of ten locomotives was built in 1939–40 but these were streamlined and now the war had started.

It's also interesting to note that the names by now were those of cities and not royalty. Until, that is, the planned 46244 *City of Leeds* was changed at the last minute to *King George VI* (4-6248 later becoming *City of Leeds*). Rather strangely the batch of four built during the war were still built with streamlining despite the need for steel in the war effort. 4-6245 *City of London* was the first of this small batch. In 1944 another batch of four was built, un-streamlined; the problems with smoke hanging over the footplate was cured when smoke deflectors were fitted.

Charles Fairburn took over as Chief Mechanical Engineer on Sir William Stanier's retirement but died in office, leaving George Ivatt as CME to upgrade the last two locomotives in the class and the last one to be built before nationalisation. This was 4-6256 and it was named in honour of Sir William, who actually named it himself *Sir William A. Stanier FRS*. The final member of the class was built at Crewe Works for British Railways in May 1948, 46257 *City of Salford*, and amazingly neither of these last two upgraded machines was preserved. *City of Salford* was scrapped at Arnott Young, Troon, in December 1964 and *Sir William A. Stanier FRS* in the same year at Cashmore's of Great Bridge.

5MT 4-6-0 No. 45021
This Stanier-designed Black Five was built at the Vulcan Foundry in August
1934 and withdrawn in September 1967 from 5B, Crewe South, then
scrapped at Cashmore's of Great Bridge three months later. It is seen here
heading north out of Warrington in 1962 with a passenger train. The line
joining on the right is the low level LNWR line.

Black Five 4-6-0 No. 45399
Travelling leisurely light engine near Leyland, south of Preston in 1965 is
Black Five 45399. The engine was built at Armstrong Whitworth in August
1937. Its last shed was 11A Carnforth, from where it was withdrawn on
31 December 1966 and cut up at Drapers, Neptune Street Goods Yard, Hull.

Jubilee Class 4-6-0 No. 45577 *Bengal*
Shrewsbury MPD now and it's 1963 as 45577 enters the turntable. The
locomotive was built at the North British Locomotive Company in Glasgow
during September 1934. The last shed was this one, where it had been
stationed since October 1961 and from where it was withdrawn in September
1964 and scrapped at Birds of Morriston in February 1965.

Royal Scot Class 4-6-0 No. 46140 *The Kings Royal Rifle Corps*
Another powerful passenger express engine now on goods duties in this case with a train of Conflat short wheelbase container wagons, as it heads south at Moore Lane Bridge south of Warrington in 1964. It is not in the best condition but considering that the whole class was withdrawn by the end of 1965 it is to be expected. Designed by Fowler and rebuilt by Stanier, it was originally built in October 1927 by the North British Locomotive Company in Glasgow. Withdrawn from Carlisle Kingmoor TMD in October 1965 and cut up five months later at J. McWilliams of Shettleston.

Jubilee Class 4-6-0 No. 45577 *Bengal*
Another look at Jubilee 45577 sitting quietly in Shrewsbury shed in 1963, it stands over the pit complete with the yellow cab side stripe.

Coronation Class 4-6-2 No. 46252 *City of Leicester*

Here we have one of William Stanier's powerful Coronation Class locomotives as it stands at the head of its train at Warrington Bank Quay station in 1962. The trainspotter is noting the details at the same time as having a chat with the driver.

On 19 November 1951, the locomotive was traversing from the fast line on to the slow line in Polesworth station when it became derailed. The engine passed through the station with the side in contact with the platform, and when it reached the end it was thrown onto its side. Seven of the train's twelve coaches left the rails but remained upright. Amazingly, there was no serious injury.

The locomotive was built in June 1944 at Crewe Works; its first allocation was 5A Crewe North. It was withdrawn on 31 May 1963 from 1B Camden and scrapped at Crewe Works on 30 September 1963.

Manor Class 4-6-0 No. 7801 *Anthony Manor*
In steam and at Oswestry MPD in 1964 is this Collett-designed Manor Class engine 7801 *Anthony Manor*. It was built at Swindon Works for the GWR, going into service in January 1938. Withdrawn from 84G Shrewsbury on 10 July 1965 and scrapped at Birds of Morriston in October 1966, it was a small class of just thirty engines, of which nine have been preserved.

Black Five No. 44917
An action shot of an engine being turned by the crew and yard staff in 1963 – they plainly enjoy a joke or two as they haul the turntable round. The shed is at Shrewsbury. The Black Five was built at Crewe Works in December 1945, and the last allocation was 5B Crewe South. From here, it was withdrawn in November 1967 and cut up at Cashmore's of Great Bridge in March 1968.

Jubilee Class 4-6-0 No. 45699 *Galatea*
45699 *Galatea* sets off southbound from Hereford station in May 1963 with its attractive train of maroon carriages. Also waiting to depart from the station are two GWR engines – Hereford had a shared shed for LMS and GWR. *Galatea* was one of the lucky Jubilees that was preserved and is still with us, it was named after *HMS Galatea*. Built in April 1936 at Crewe Works and withdrawn from 84G Shrewsbury in November 1964. In 1953, the engine was derailed and ended up on its side. Despite this, only two people were slightly injured and very slight damage was done to the engine. After withdrawal and a short spell at Eastleigh it was taken to Barry scrapyard in January 1965. It remained there slowly deteriorating until 1980, when it was rescued by the late Brian Oliver and moved to the Severn Valley Railway. The original plan was for it to be a donor engine for 45690 *Leander* that was being rebuilt. It ended up at Steamtown at Carnforth, where it was given a total rebuild and returned to mainline steam in April 2013. *Galatea* is currently heading steam specials on the main line and is painted in British Rail maroon.

Jubilee Class 4-6-0 No. 45699 *Galatea*
Here is *Galatea* at Shrewsbury station in 1965. Not in the best condition but not too bad for 1965.

Castle Class 4-6-0 No. 7020 *Gloucester Castle*
A look at a member of the Castle Class now as it sits cold at the 84B Oxley GWR shed in 1963. Despite the run-down appearance of the surroundings, Oxley shed would remain in service to see a new generation of locomotives pass through its doors. This locomotive, however, was not so lucky; it already looks neglected. This is probably because it was destined to be scrapped the following year. It was designed by Charles Collett and built by the GWR at Swindon Works in May 1949. It was withdrawn from 81C Southall on 30 September 1964 (I suspect that it was here on the scrap line albeit on Southall's books) and scrapped at R.S. Hayes/Birds, Tremains Yard, Bridgend on 31 December 1964.

Castle Class 4-6-0 No. 4079 *Pendennis Castle*

This beautifully prepared engine arrives at Shrewsbury station, from London Paddington, with a special on a wet Sunday, 26 September 1965. The engine was built in February 1924 at Swindon Works. It was withdrawn on 5 May 1964 from 82B St Philips Marsh and was purchased from British Rail the same year. More on this locomotive later.

Snowdon mountain railway rack engine 0-4-2T No. 6 *Padarn*

Not mainline steam, but interesting all the same is this shot of *'Padarn'* of the Snowdon Mountain Railway being made ready to tackle the climb to the top in 1962. This engine was built in 1922 by the Swiss Locomotive and Machine Works in Winterthur and is still in service today. The line was constructed between 1894 and 1896 and travels from Llanberis to the summit of Mount Snowdon, the highest mountain in Wales. It is the only rack and pinion railway in Great Britain.

Unnamed Black Five

No number here, but the glorious array of semaphore signals combined with the pure steam era ambiance makes this photo well deserving of a place. The engine and its mixed goods departs Derby station in 1962, leaving behind well-dressed trainspotters busily marking off the number of the Black Five in their Ian Allan books. The man nearest the camera is in possession of a very common bag of the period – a Second World War gas mask case. The engine hauls its train past one of the two engine sidings signal boxes at this busy station. Both have now gone, but what a great photograph!

Manor Class GWR 4-6-0 No. 7819 *Hinton Manor*

Photographed on a wet day in 1965, this atmospheric shot shows the driver, or perhaps the fireman, patiently waiting the off from Shrewsbury station. The engine is scruffy and unkempt but this would one day change. It was designed by C.B. Collett and built at Swindon Works in 1939, allocated to 87G Carmarthen on nationalisation; the last shed was 84G Shrewsbury, from where it was withdrawn in 1965.

Manor Class GWR 4-6-0 No. 7819 *Hinton Manor*
This was one of the lucky engines, sent to Woodham Brothers in Barry, from where it was eventually rescued in 1973 by the Hinton Manor Fund aided by the Severn Valley Railway, where it joined two classmates, *Erlestoke Manor* and *Bradley Manor*. It was restored and returned to the main line in 1977. After travelling many miles on the SVR and main line it is now owned by the Severn Valley Railway Charitable Trust and at the time of writing is a static exhibition within the Swindon Designer Outlet of McArthur Glen, once the Swindon Railway Works!

Standard Class 4 4-6-0 No. 75004 departs Barmouth station in 1964
A look now at a scene that includes the period surrounds of Barmouth station complete with large advertisements, as Standard Class 4 trundles beneath the station footbridge on one of the through lines. The Riddles-designed engine was built at Swindon Works in August 1951. On 9 January 1966 it was allocated to Shrewsbury, from where it was withdrawn in March 1967. Five months later it was cut up at Cashmore's of Newport.

9F 2-10-0 No. 92121
Bilston Street railway station, Willenhall, on the Walsall to Wolverhampton line, was closed in 1965. Here No. 92121 passes through with a heavy train in 1966. The 9F was built in February 1957; its last shed was 6C Birkenhead, from where it was withdrawn, after just ten years' service in July 1967. It was cut up at T.J. Thompson & Sons of Stockton in January 1968.

GWR 0-6-2 Tank 5697 of the 5600 Class
Built to the design of C.B. Collett, these numerous engines of 5600 Class were built between 1924 and 1928. This one, No. 5697, is seen at the rear of Oswestry shed in early 1963 shortly before or after withdrawal. Built at Swindon Works by the GWR on the 31 January 1927. In July 1960 it was sent to 88A Radyr, from where it was withdrawn on 4 April 1963 and scrapped at Cashmore's of Newport in December of the same year. These small but heavy locomotives were a favourite of the Welsh lines.

Fowler 0-6-0 No. 43967

Another large class of engines, the Fowler 0-6-0, is a true workhorse of steam railways. No. 43967 is seen here at Derby station in 1962 with one of the engine sidings signal boxes at the rear. The engine was built in January 1922 by Armstrong Whitworth. Its last shed was 9D Buxton, from where it was withdrawn in August 1965. It was scrapped in December of that year at Birds Bynea scrapyard.

Standard 4MT 4-6-0 No. 75029

Seen here at Barmouth station in 1964 with a period view of a small station in this year, we see a Standard 4MT engine with a short local train. This Riddles-designed engine was built at Swindon Works in May 1954 and in 1957 acquired a double chimney. Its last shed was 5D Stoke, from where it was withdrawn on 31 August 1967. This lucky engine avoided the cutters torch when it was one of the locomotives bought by the artist and conservationist, David Shepherd, the same year. Initially it was taken to the short-lived Longmoor Steam Railway. In 1973, it was then delivered to the East Somerset Railway and since the late 1990s it has been at the North Yorkshire Moors Railway. The engine, now in British Rail green, has been named *The Green Knight* and at the time of writing, is currently in for repair.

Britannia Class 4-6-2 No. 70025 *Western Star*
Another look at this Brit, but this time in Preston station during 1966 with a goods train and plenty of leaking steam. It was built at Crewe Works during September 1952 and allocated to 86C Cardiff Canton. The last shed was 68A Carlisle Kingmoor, from where it was withdrawn on 23 December 1967 and cut up at Campbells of Airdrie the following month.

SR Merchant Navy Class Pacific 4-6-2 No. 35030 *Elder Dempster Lines*
Here we see a modified Bulleid design Merchant Navy Class Pacific passing Eastleigh Works in 1965 with an interesting rake of carriages. The locomotive was built at Eastleigh Works during April 1949 and modernised with the casing removed in April 1958. It was withdrawn from 70A Nine Elms in July 1967 and scrapped at J. Buttigiegs of Newport during November 1968. This engine was the last to pull a main line train using steam on the SR, hauling the 14.11 Weymouth to Waterloo train on 9 July 1967. Eleven members of the class were preserved but not this one, the last to be withdrawn.

Manor Class 4-6-0 No. 7821 *Ditcheat Manor*

This smart Collett-designed engine seems to be reversing in the Oxley area during 1963 as the driver and fireman look back along the train. It was built at Swindon Works in November 1950 for BR and the last shed was 84G Shrewsbury, from where it was withdrawn on 30 November 1965. Not for the cutters torch but to be sent to Woodham Brothers scrapyard at Barry, from where it was rescued in 1980. After a period of restoration, it was steamed in 1998. It moved to several preservation sites, eventually ending up on the West Somerset Railway when in 2007 they bought it from its private owner. Due to the extensive work required it was agreed that it could be taken to the GWR Museum at Swindon, where it still resides as a static exhibit.

Castle Class 4-6-0 No. 4079 *Pendennis Castle*

Shrewsbury on 25 September 1965 as 4079 *Pendennis Castle* enters the station to collect passengers and entertain enthusiasts. It is at the head of special 1X82 from Paddington. The ten-coach special was organised by Ian Allan for the Talyllyn Preservation Society. It took place over 25 and 26 September 1965 and conveyed people to the Talyllyn AGM. The journey was from London Paddington and back on assorted routes using Locomotives D 1684, 7802 and 7812 plus *Pendennis Castle*.

No. 4079 was built at Swindon Works, going into service in March 1924. It was withdrawn from 82B St Philip's Marsh in May 1964. Bought by Mike Higson from British Rail, between then and 1977 it suffered a rollercoaster of pride and pain before eventually being bought by Hammersley Iron in

Australia with the intention of running it on their private Hammersley Iron network. It was subjected to urgent work and then a final run on British Rail track at the head of the 'Great Western Envoy' special from Birmingham to Didcot and return. The following day it was to Avonmouth and the SS *Mishraf* for delivery to Australia, where it had a reunion with *Flying Scotsman* on 17 September 1989. Its final run in Australia was on 14 October 1994. More problems resulted in the locomotive being stored for some time until an arrangement was made with the Great Western Society to whom it was donated by Rio Tinto, who were now at the helm

It was shipped to Bristol in 2000 and to the Didcot Railway Centre, where restoration was later started and is, at the time of writing, still underway.

Stanier Class 4 2-6-4 Tank No. 42611

Another possible station pilot or one awaiting a local train allocation at Crewe station in 1962 is this British Rail workhorse No. 42611. It was built at the North British Locomotive Works in Glasgow in 1937 and withdrawn from 10D Lostock Hall in March 1967, then cut up at Cashmore's of Great Bridge in September of that year.

Manor Class 4-6-0 No. 7828 *Odney Manor*

A once powerful Collett-designed GWR Manor Class engine that is now acting as the station shunter at Shrewsbury. It is 1965 and the engine has just a few months before withdrawal; it was built at Swindon Works and went into BR service in December 1950. It was withdrawn from 6D Shrewsbury on 2 October 1965 and was one of the lucky engines sent to Woodhams yard in Barry, South Wales, the following year. In 1981, it was purchased privately from Woodhams and taken to the Gloucestershire Warwickshire Railway, where it underwent a full restoration and returned to the rails. In 2004, it was sold to the West Somerset Railway and on 7 June 2011 it was renamed *Norton Manor*, a tribute to 40 Commando whose base is by the WSR in Norton Fitzwarren and the name of a GWR Manor that was ordered and cancelled.

Standard Class 4 4-6-0 75032

In a very scruffy state with a strange front number plate this Riddles-designed Standard 4 is seen at Preston station in late 1965. In July 1963 it was allocated to 27A Bank Hall and still displays the name on the buffer beam. At the time of photographing, was recently reallocated to 5D Stoke. The locomotive was built at Swindon Works, going into service in June 1953. In February 1968 it was withdrawn from 10A Carnforth and scrapped three months later at T.W. Ward of Beighton.

Fairburn 2-6-4 Tank No. 42081

Seen at 9E Trafford Park MPD in 1965 in steam and with a full tender is this Fairburn-designed 3-6-4 Tank engine. Built at Brighton Works during January 1951 and allocated to 73A Stewarts Lane. The last shed was this one, from where it was withdrawn in May 1967 and broken up at Cashmore's of Great Bridge in November of that year.

9F 2-10-0 No. 92120
In a state that locomotives were allowed to become, this five-year-old 9F is seen at Derby MPD in 1962. It was built at Crewe Works in 1957 and withdrawn from 8H Birkenhead Mollington Street in July 1967, to be cut up at Birds of Long Marston during February 1968.

Jinty 0-6-0 Tank No. 47472
Seen giving a little assistance to 9F 2-10-0 92116, at Preston station in 1966. The little Jinty was built at the Vulcan Foundry, going into service in December 1927. After a long life, it was withdrawn from 24C Lostock Hall in November 1966 and scrapped at T.W. Ward, Beighton, Sheffield, in March 1967. The relatively new Riddles 9F was built at Crewe Works during December 1956 and withdrawn from 8B Warrington Dallam on 30 November 1966, and then scrapped at Drapers, Neptune Street Goods Yard on 31 July 1967.

Jubilee Class 4-6-0 No. 45617 *Mauritius*
Alongside the platform No. 45617 is awaiting a new roster as the driver and fireman look out of the cab at Crewe station in 1962. The locomotive was built at Crewe Works in 1934 and withdrawn from 5A Crewe North in November 1964, to be scrapped at T.W. Ward of Beighton, Sheffield, four months later.

Jubilee Class 4-6-0 No. 45611 *Hong Kong*
Seen at Derby MPD in 1962 is a relatively clean Jubilee 45611 *Hong Kong*. Built at Crewe Works in 1934 and withdrawn from this MPD in September 1964 to be cut up at Cashmore's of Great Bridge in January 1965.

Class N15 0-6-2 Tank No. 69211
It is 64F Bathgate MPD, Edinburgh in 1962 and Class N15 stands cold and unloved. The engine was designed by William Patton Reid and built at Cowlairs Works for the NBR in 1923. It was withdrawn from 64B Haymarket in October 1962 and scrapped at P.W. McLellan of Coatbridge in June 1964.

Gresley A4 4-6-2 No. 60004 *William Whitelaw*
It is 30 June 1963 and the Railway Correspondence and Travel Society (West Riding Branch) are on the 'Three Summit Rail Tour' headed by 60004 *William Whitelaw*, assisted at various locations by 46255 *City of Hereford*, 3F 57581 and 60023 *Golden Eagle*. The tour was from Leeds City to Carlisle and taking in Scottish lines and returning over Shap. No. 60004 was designed by Gresley and built at Doncaster Works in December 1937. Its last shed was 61B Aberdeen Ferryhill, from where it was withdrawn in July 1966 and scrapped at the Motherwell Machinery and Scrap of Inslow Works, Wishaw.

Black Five 4-6-0 No. 45181
The location is not known but the date is 1965. The engine was built at Armstrong Whitworth in September 1935. Its last shed was 8C Speke Junction, as shown on the buffer bar. It was withdrawn from there in January 1966 and scrapped at Cashmore's of Great Bridge four months later.

J36 Class 0-6-0 No. 65282
Bathgate MPD in Scotland during 1962, and we see a truly ancient locomotive. Designed by Mathew Holmes, Locomotive Superintendent of the North British Railway from 1882 to 1903. This engine was one of his designs and it was built at Cowlairs Works in Scotland during November 1896. It was rebuilt in May 1922. It was withdrawn from this MPD in January 1966 and scrapped at Motherwell Machinery and Scrap of Wishaw on 4 April 1966.

Jubilee Class 4-6-0 No. 45596 *Bahamas*
It is Stockport Edgeley MPD and No. 45596 is being cleaned for an enthusiast's excursion on 4 December 1965. It was the RCTS (Lancs and North West Branch) and the locomotives involved were 45596 *Bahamas* and 45654 *Hood*. The route from Crewe to Manchester Exchange was covered by *Bahamas*. Then *Hood* took the train from Liverpool Lime Street to Manchester Exchange and then the train was joined and the two engines double-headed took it on to York. The return journey mirrored the outwards one. *Bahamas* was built in January 1935 by the North British Locomotive Company in Glasgow. It was withdrawn from this MPD on 23 March 1966 and purchased from British Rail in January of the following year by the newly formed Bahamas Locomotive Society. At the time of writing it can be found undergoing a major boiler overhaul at Tyseley Locomotive Works but will shortly be back on the main line. *Hood* was built at Crewe Works in February 1935 and was withdrawn from 26A Newton Heath on 25 June 1966 and scrapped at T.W. Ward of Beighton, Sheffield, four months later.

Royal Scot Class 4-6-0 No. 46115 *Scots Guardsman*
Already featured in the book on the RCTS 'Rebuilt Scot Commemorative Tour', 1X80 and now the tour reaches Carlisle station in 1965.

Fowler 0-6-0 Tank No. 47677
It is the parcels platform at Crewe station in 1964 and a Jinty, probably a station pilot, has stopped at the platform with a train of parcel vans. The engine was built at Horwich Works during August 1931 and its last allocation was 5B Crewe South. It was scrapped five months later at Cashmore's of Great Bridge.

Britannia Pacific 4-6-2 No. 70025 *Western Star*
A close-up view of a once-proud locomotive in the run up to the end of steam on British Rail. It's Preston station in 1966 and this shot is of the front of *Western Star* with its hand-painted name. Note the handgrips on the windshields: they were put there when the handrails were removed for safety reasons, having been blamed for a previous accident caused by the visibility being impeded by said handrails.

Highland Railway 4-6-0 Jones Goods 103

Taken at Dawsholm MPD, situated in the Kelvindale area of Glasgow, in early 1964 is this ancient and beautiful locomotive. The class were designed as goods engines by the Highland Railways Locomotive Superintendent David Jones, and built by Sharp, Stewart and Company, Atlas Works, Glasgow. There were just fifteen locomotives in the class, delivered between September and November 1894. They were the first British-designed locomotives with the wheel arrangement 4-6-0. When built they were known as the HR Big Goods Class and in 1900 became Class 1. At the time they were the most powerful main line locomotives in Great Britain.

When the Highland Railway became part of the LMS the class were classified as 4F and all were withdrawn between 1929 and 1940 – only this one was preserved. It was returned to working order by British Railways in 1959 and spent many years operating enthusiast specials. In 1965, it starred in the film *Those Magnificent Men in their Flying Machines*. In 1966, it finally retired and can now be found in the Glasgow Museum of Transport. The Dawsholm MPD was a brick-built six-road dead-end shed, with a twin track repair shop. It became a base for preserved Scottish locomotives and closed on 3 October 1964.

Britannia Class 4-6-2 No. 70014 *Iron Duke*
Preston station in late 1964 and stopped at the platform is
70014 *Iron Duke* with a parcels train. Coming up on the
outside is Class 2 2-6-0 No. 78002. Both locomotives were
detailed earlier in the book, but are worth another look.

The Caledonian Railway Caley single 4-2-2 No. 123
Again at 65D Dawsholm MPD in early 1964 when these
ancient locomotives were put on display for the press.
No. 123 was built by Neilson and Company in 1886 as an
exhibition locomotive. It became part of the Caledonian
Railway in 1914 and the LMS in 1923, when it was given the
number 123. It worked the Directors Saloon until 1930 when
it went back into general service, and was withdrawn in 1935
to be taken into preservation. British Rail restored it in 1958
and it was used on classic trains until Scottish steam was
withdrawn. Like the Jones Goods it can be found on display
at the Glasgow Museum of Transport.

4-4-0 No. 49 *Gordon Highlander*
Still at Dawsholm in 1964 and we see No. 49 *Gordon Highlander* or, as the Scots call it, *The Sojer*. It was built at the North British Locomotive Company in 1920 for the Great North of Scotland Railway. At grouping it was given the number 6849, later 2277, and on amalgamation in 1946 of BR the number 62277. On 13 June 1964 it worked the Carlisle and Silloth leg of the 'Solway Ranger Railtour'. It was eventually withdrawn and became a static exhibit at the Glasgow Transport Museum, but in 2011 it was sent on loan to the Scottish Railway Preservation Society Museum at Bo'ness, West Lothian, Scotland.

The storage roads at Dallam MPD, Warrington
Just a brief look between the lines of engines parked up on the storage road at Dallam MPD circa 1965. You can get an idea of the fun it was to walk through railway sheds and yards during the steam period.

B-B 4 Warship Class No. D832 *Onslaught*

The year is 1962 and steam traction is slowly being usurped by diesel and electric. In the West Country the main infiltrators were engines from the Warship Class of diesel hydraulics. Here we see one such at Penzance in Cornwall. The locomotive was built at Swindon Works and introduced in February 1962. It was withdrawn in December 1972 and went into British Rail Research at Derby, and it then to the Bury Transport Museum. It is one of only two of the class to be preserved and at the time of writing can be found on the East Lancashire Railway Diesel Group.

2-6-4 Tanks No. 42210 and one other

A pair of Fairburn Class 4s returning from banking duties on the Shap incline in 1965. The lead engine is No. 42210 and it was built at Derby Works during December 1945. Its last shed was 11D Tebay, from where it was withdrawn on 6 May 1967 and scrapped at J. McWilliams of Shettleston, five months later.

J37 Class 0-6-0's Nos 64623 and 64633

On Bathgate MPD in 1962 we see two William Patton Reid-designed J37 locomotives. No. 64623 was built in January 1921 by the North British Locomotive Company, Glasgow, for the NBR. It was withdrawn from 62B Dundee Tay Bridge in November 1966 and scrapped at Campbells of Airdrie three months later. No. 64633 was built at Cowlairs Works in 1921 and withdrawn from 65A Eastfield during June 1964 for scrapping at Motherwell Machinery and Scrap at Wishaw four months later.

Standard Class 3 2-6-0 No. 77000

This must be one of the saddest images in the book, of a relatively new engine in a shocking state. Here the Standard is seen at Stourton MPD in 1964. It was designed by Riddles and at this time would have been in service for only nine years. Despite the condition and derelict situation, it is in steam. Behind it is an attractive old Gresley coach. The locomotive was built at Swindon Works, going into service in February 1954 at 51A Darlington. It was allocated to Stourton in June 1964, from where it was withdrawn on 7 December 1966 and scrapped at T.W. Ward of Beighton, Sheffield, in March 1967.

5MT 4-6-0 No. 44877
Seen stopped at Heaton Mersey station with a goods train in 1964 is this tidy looking Black Five. Someone has pinched the shed plate but other than that it looks intact. The locomotive was built at Crewe Works and went into service in April 1945. Withdrawn from 10A Carnforth on the last day of regular steam, 3 August 1968, it was scrapped at Cohens of Kettering four months later.

Merchant Navy Class No. 35008 *Orient Line*
Here we have a Bulleid-designed locomotive built at Eastleigh Works in June 1942. It was built as a streamlined 'Spam Can' and the casing was removed in 1957. It was withdrawn from 70A Nine Elms on 9 July 1967 and scrapped at J. Buttegeig of Newport the following year. It is seen here in 1965 at Weymouth MPD.

WD 2-8-0 No. 90684
One of Riddles excellent locomotives built for the WD, in this case at the
Vulcan Foundry in 1944 with the number 79221. In 1948 it was bought
by British Rail from the War Department and renumbered 90684. It is seen
here at Normanton in 1965, at the time it was based at 56A Wakefield, from
where it was withdrawn on 31 January 1967 and scrapped four months later
at Cox & Danks of Wadsley Bridge.

Jubilee Class 4-6-0 No. 45660 *Rooke*
Another sad sight, this time of Jubilee *Rooke* at Leeds Holbeck in 1966,
minus names and smokebox number. This once beautiful engine has been
withdrawn and awaits the cutters torch. It was built at Derby Works in
December 1934 and started its active life here. That life also ended here
when it was withdrawn on 31 June 1966 and cut up at Drapers, Neptune
Street Goods Yard in Hull just three months later.

Jubilee Class 4-6-0 No. 45581 *Bihar and Orissa*
Seen at Farnley Junction MPD in 1966. It was allocated to this MPD in 1957, where it remained for the rest of its active days. It was withdrawn from here in August 1966 and stored for a while, before being cut up at Drapers, Neptune Street Goods Yard in Hull in December of that year. The engine had been built in 1934 at the North British Locomotive Works in Glasgow. One incident of note was when it was hauling the Leeds–Edinburgh Express on 11 October 1943. Passing between Steeton and Silsden in Yorkshire, it collided with a goods train being shunted. It was a serious accident with the train ending up on its side but, fortunately, there were no fatalities and only four minor injuries.

Jubilee Class 4-6-0 No. 45647 *Sturdee*
At Dallam shed now in Warrington and still complete with name plate looking original is Jubilee 45647 *Sturdee*. The year is 1965 and the engine is sooty but quite clean for the era. It was built at Crewe Works in January 1935 and the last shed was 20A Leeds Holbeck, from where it was withdrawn in April 1967 and scrapped at Cashmore's of Great Bridge four months later.

Jubilee Class 4-6-0 No. 45565 *Victoria*
Seen on Stockport Edgeley MPD in 1965, a stranger in the form
of Jubilee 4-6-0 *Victoria* with the number 1M91, which usually
indicates a Plymouth to Liverpool train. The engine is in very good
cosmetic condition complete with a hand-painted name. The
locomotive was built by the North British Locomotive Company in
Glasgow during August 1934 and the last allocation was 25F Low
Moor, from where it was withdrawn in January 1967. It was cut
up at Drapers, Neptune Street Goods Yard, on 19 June 1967.

Steam climbs over Shap
Here we see just how beautiful Britain is as we look down on the
Shap line at what appears to be a steam banker, banking a diesel
up the incline in 1966.

WD 2-8-0 No. 90680

Another example of just how badly cared for locomotives were towards the end of steam. Seen here at Mirfield shed in late 1966 and looking very work-stained and uncared for is an engine built at the Vulcan Foundry for the War Department and going into service in January 1944. No. 90680 was bought in October 1949 from the War Department by British Rail and given this number. It was withdrawn from 55D Royston in January 1967 and cut up at T.W. Ward of Killamarsh in May of that year. This is probably the worst example of neglect in the book.

WD 2-8-0 No. 90337 with Black Five No. 44896

Seen here is a pleasant view of what seems a small MPD but at its height employed 200 men – the shed is now not part of the railway. It's 1966 and the locomotive on view alongside the shed is No. 44896 which has already featured in this book in somewhat better condition. The War Department engine 90337 was built for the War Department in August 1944 and brought into British Rail in 1949, then given this number. It was withdrawn from 21D Normanton in January 1967, being scrapped at Cox & Danks of Wadsley Bridge seven months later.

Britannia Class 4-6-2 No. 70047
One of the two unnamed Britannia Pacifics, No. 70047, was frequently on specials over Southern rails during the 1960s. Here it can be seen in Eastleigh shed in 1965. It was built at Crewe Works during June 1954. Its last shed was 68A Carlisle Kingmoor, from where it was withdrawn on 29 July 1967 and scrapped at Campbells of Airdrie five months later.

Royal Scot Class 4-6-0 No. 46155 *The Lancer*
In 1964 Crewe station platforms were a favourite with enthusiasts and here a good 'cop' is seen in the form of a Royal Scot No. 46155 built during July 1930 at Derby Works. Its last shed was 68A Carlisle Kingmoor, from where it was withdrawn on 12 December 1964 and scrapped at Arnott Young of Troon two months later.

4-6-2 60021 *Wild Swan*

This Gresley-designed A4 engine is seen at speed near
Doncaster in 1963 with a line of maroon coaches. The
smart Brunswick green paint is fading and the engine does
not have long to go. Built at Doncaster Works during 1938
for the LNER, its last allocation was 34E New England, from
where it was withdrawn on 20 October 1963 and then
scrapped at Doncaster Works in January 1964.

**Standard Class 3 2-6-0 No. 77000 and Britannia Class
4-6-2 No. 70053** *Moray Firth*

It is 20B Stourton MPD, Leeds in 1966 and the engines
here, although unkempt, are at least in steam. The first one
is the Riddles 3MT 77000 which featured earlier. The other
Riddles engine, *Moray Firth*, was built at Crewe Works in
September 1954. Its last shed was 68A Carlisle Kingmoor,
from where it was withdrawn on 15 April 1967 and
scrapped at J. McWilliams of Shettleston five months later.

Two English Electric Type 4s bring a passenger train into Crewe station in 1962
A quick look at Crewe station now as diesels start to take over in 1962. Spotters watching are thankful that at least one of them has been named.

No. 46115 *Scots Guardsman*
Here we have a good shot of a very tidy Royal Scot at Hellifield station. The date is 13 February 1965 and the engine is at the head of the RCTS 'Rebuilt Scot Commemorative Tour'. No. 46115 was assisted by Black Five 44822 Crewe to Wigan with No. 46115, Wigan to Blackburn double-headed, Blackburn to Carlisle and return to Crewe 46115 and 44822. The latter was built at Derby Works during December 1944 and withdrawn from 26A Newton Heath on 31 October 1967, before being scrapped at Cashmore's of Newport on 31 May 1968.

Jinty 0-6-0T No. 47326
It's 1965 and this ubiquitous Jinty is on station pilot duty at Carlisle station shunting a single oil tank with a nice maroon carriage in the shot. The Jinty was built at the North British Locomotive Company of Glasgow during July 1926 and was withdrawn from 12A Carlisle Kingmoor on 3 April 1965 but reallocated to 10D Lostock Hall then sent for scrapping at J. McWilliams of Shettlestone on 30 September 1967.

No. 46115 *Scots Guardsman*
Another look now at the 'Rebuilt Scot Commemorative Tour' in 1965, this time at Carlisle station during train marshalling. It is still three years before the end of steam but look at the number of enthusiasts here to watch a smart engine and its train pass through. The government of the time underestimated the interest in steam as they worked tirelessly to scrap as many as they could, including this one.

Ivatt Tank Class 2MT, 2-6-2 41222
Carlisle station in 1965 and this photograph shows the extensive track layout to the south of the station. The engine, looking lonely on its own, was built during October 1948 at Crewe Works. The last shed was 68A Carlisle Kingmoor, from where it was withdrawn on 31 December 1966 and cut up at J. McWilliams of Shettleston on 30 September 1967.

Jubilee class 4-6-0 No. 45552 *Silver Jubilee*

Oh, how the mighty fall as we see a dirty 4-6-0 number 45552 *Silver Jubilee* as it heads a short parcels train northbound at Winwick Junction north of Warrington in 1963. This famous engine was built at Crewe Works in June 1934 as No. 5552 The following April it swapped identities with 5642 that had been built in December 1935 (5642 was later named *Boscawen*). *Silver Jubilee* was the first of what came to be known as the Jubilee Class. It was given special treatment. The Jubilees were painted in crimson lake (red) but 5552 was repainted in all over black with silver lining. It was given specially cast chrome numbers and named *Silver Jubilee* to mark the Silver Jubilee of King George V. It remained like this until its first allocation at nationalisation, which was 9A Longsight, at which time it was renumbered 45552. Its last shed was Crewe North and it was withdrawn

on 26 September 1964 and cut up at Cashmore's of Great Bridge on 31 January 1965.

Whatever the condition of the engine at withdrawal, the person who made the decision to scrap such an iconic engine did no one any favours. Since the demise of the engine, other preserved engines have been disguised as it, for instance, 45593 *Kolhapur* was painted in the original livery to mark the Silver Jubilee of the preserved Great Central Railway during 2003. Jubilee 45690 *Leander* was temporarily renamed *Silver Jubilee* to celebrate the Silver Jubilee of Her Majesty Queen Elizabeth II, though it remained in crimson red livery. Model makers Bachman Branchline have an 00 gauge model of *Silver Jubilee*. *Silver Jubilee* joins the list of important locomotives such as *Sir William A. Stanier FRS* – iconic in their own right, but still ordered to be scrapped.

8F 2-8-0 No. 48665 and Standard Class 4
Now at Croes Newydd MPD in Wrexham in 1966, the
Stanier 8F and an unnamed Class 4 are surrounded
by the detritus of an old steam shed. We have already
detailed this engine when allocated here, but it would
soon be on the move, ending up near to the end of
steam at 10F Rose Grove, where it was withdrawn on
the last official day of steam, 3 August 1968.

8F 2-8-0 No. 48618
Entering Preston station with a southbound freight in
1966 is 8F 48618, a massive class of successful Stanier
workhorses. No. 48618 was built at Ashford Works for
the Southern Region during 1943 and was withdrawn
from 10D Lostock Hall in October 1967 for scrapping.

A steam-hauled freight
No numbers here but a nice photo looking into the distance as a goods train heads north towards Warrington, over the Manchester Ship Canal, in 1962.

Standard Class 4 2-6-0, No. 76033
Allocated to 70D Eastleigh but seen here at 70G Weymouth receiving repairs. Separated from the tender and with the back end supported by a crane, work seems to be under way necessitating the removal of some wheels that can be seen on the adjoining line. The engine was built at Doncaster Works during December 1953 and the last shed was 70C Guildford, from where it was withdrawn in January 1967 and scrapped at Cashmore's of Newport during September 1967.

Standard Class 4 2-6-0 No. 76007
Standard Class 4 76007 takes water on Weymouth MPD in 1965. This engine was built at Horwich Works going into service in January 1953. It was withdrawn from 70F Bournemouth in July 1967 and scrapped at Birds of Morriston four months later. This locomotive is featured again later in the book.

9F 2-10-0 No. 92107
At Shrewsbury station in 1966 and a Riddles 9F is passing through with a train of tank wagons. The Riddles-designed engine was built at Crewe Works during September 1956. It was withdrawn from 6C Birkenhead on 28 February 1967 and scrapped at Drapers, Neptune Street Goods Yard, Hull, five months later.

Ivatt Class 4 2-6-0 No. 43031
Seen at Manchester Central station in 1964 is Ivatt engine 43031, probably acting as station pilot. It was built at Horwich Works during April 1949 and was withdrawn from 13C Heaton Mersey on 12 March 1966. Scrapping came three months later at the Central Wagon Company of Ince, Wigan, in June the same year.

9F 2-10-0 No. 92135
At Croes Newydd MPD in 1965 and 9F No. 92135 is parked near to an old carriage marked Loco Carriage & Wagon Dept. Croes Newydd. The Riddles 9F is not in bad condition but then again it is quite new, having been built at Crewe Works during June 1957. It was withdrawn from 25A Wakefield on 30 June 1967 and cut up at Drapers Neptune Street Goods Yard, Hull, in March 1968 when nine years and eleven months old.

West Country Class 4-6-2 No. 34040 *Crewkerne*
It is Bournemouth shed in 1965 and, with numbers and name intact, WC Class 34040 is in steam with 34025 *Wimple* behind it. The Bulleid engine was built for the SR at Brighton Works, going into service in September 1946. The engine was withdrawn from this shed in September 1967 and scrapped at Cashmore's of Newport in March 1968.

WC Class 4-6-2 No. 34040 *Crewkerne*
Another look at 4-6-2 *Crewkerne* on Bournemouth shed in 1965 and a chance to take a close look at the unusual tender design on these West Country/Battle of Britain engines. This is another locomotive that has been involved in a crash. At 5.56 p.m. on 11 April 1961 an electric passenger train from Effingham Junction to Waterloo, London, ran head on into *Crewkerne*, which was running tender towards the TMD. The electric train had failed to stop for a red light and sadly the driver was killed. *Crewkerne*'s tender was derailed and destroyed.

WC Class 4-6-2 No. 34025 *Whimple*

Still at Bournemouth but this time in the MPD in 1965 and we see a Bulleid's West Country/Battle of Britain Class engine 34025 *Whimple*. Not in steam and either withdrawn or soon to be so, it was built at Brighton Works, going into service in March 1946 as *Rough Tor*. The following month *Rough Tor* was replaced with *Whimple*, named after a small village in East Devon. Originally built with air-smoothed casing and rebuilt in November 1957, it was withdrawn from this MPD in July 1967 and scrapped at Cashmore's of Newport in March 1968.

Merchant Navy Class 4-6-2 No. 35026 *Lamport and Holt Line*

It is 20 November 1966 and Bulleid 4-6-2 *Lamport and Holt Line* is seen at the head of the 'William Deacons Bank club tour' in York station. The route was from Manchester Piccadilly to York and return via a different route to Manchester Victoria. The locomotive was built at Eastleigh Works for the Southern Railway during December 1948 and rebuilt in 1957 when the casing was removed. Its last shed was 70G Weymouth Radipole from where it was withdrawn in March 1967 and cut up six months later at Cashmore's of Newport.

Standard Class 4 2-6-0 No. 76006
Sitting on one of the centre lines in the cavernous Bournemouth station in 1967 is Robert Riddles-designed Standard 76006. The locomotive was built at Horwich Works, going into service at Eastleigh during January 1953. It was withdrawn from 70F Bournemouth in July 1967 and cut up at Birds of Morriston during November 1967.

Standard Class 4 2-6-0 No. 76007
Bournemouth station in 1967 and the sister locomotive to No. 76006 is seen here at the head of a local train in Bournemouth. Built and into service in January 1953, it was withdrawn in April 1967 and also scrapped at Birds of Morriston in November 1967.

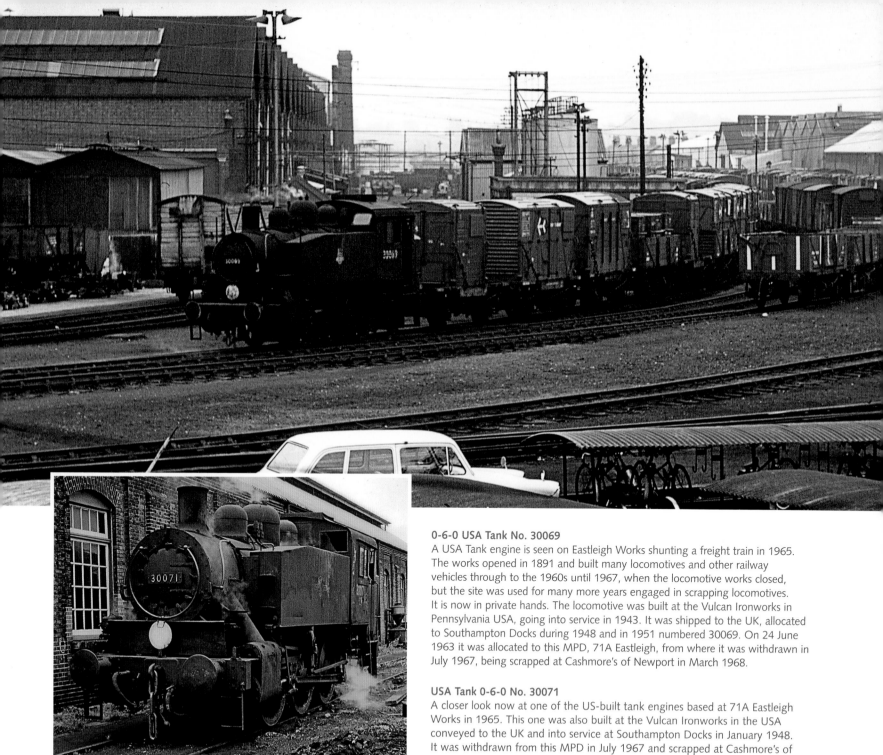

0-6-0 USA Tank No. 30069

A USA Tank engine is seen on Eastleigh Works shunting a freight train in 1965. The works opened in 1891 and built many locomotives and other railway vehicles through to the 1960s until 1967, when the locomotive works closed, but the site was used for many more years engaged in scrapping locomotives. It is now in private hands. The locomotive was built at the Vulcan Ironworks in Pennsylvania USA, going into service in 1943. It was shipped to the UK, allocated to Southampton Docks during 1948 and in 1951 numbered 30069. On 24 June 1963 it was allocated to this MPD, 71A Eastleigh, from where it was withdrawn in July 1967, being scrapped at Cashmore's of Newport in March 1968.

USA Tank 0-6-0 No. 30071

A closer look now at one of the US-built tank engines based at 71A Eastleigh Works in 1965. This one was also built at the Vulcan Ironworks in the USA conveyed to the UK and into service at Southampton Docks in January 1948. It was withdrawn from this MPD in July 1967 and scrapped at Cashmore's of Newport during March 1968.

4-4-0 No. 62712 *Morayshire* in front of No. 54398 *Ben Alder*

A look now into Dawsholm MPD in 1964, with three good 'cops'. Gresley-designed No. 62712 *Morayshire* was built at Darlington Works on 20 February 1928. It is 1964 and the engine has been here for some time, it was withdrawn from 64G Hawick on 3 July 1961. After time as a stationary boiler at Slateford Laundry in Edinburgh, it was put in store at Dalry Road, Edinburgh. After negotiations with British Rail it was moved to this MPD and later, in 1964, was hauled by *Gordon Highlander* to Inverurie Works for restoration. In 1966 it was handed over to the Royal Scottish Museum in Edinburgh who, in 1974, agreed a loan to the Scottish Railway Preservation Society for restoration. From 1975 to 1983 the engine was on the main lines based at Falkirk. In July 2003, the engine participated in an open day at Doncaster Works. At the time of writing, 62712 *Morayshire* is at the Llangollen Railway Engineering Company for overhaul and is expected back at Bo'Ness in 2018.

The engine at the rear, 54398 *Ben Alder*, was not so lucky. It was stored with *Morayshire* in preparation for being preserved but it was not to be. It was built at Dubs & Company during July 1898 and withdrawn from 60D Wick on 31 March 1953. After years of being stored, it was scrapped at the Motherwell Machinery and Scrap, Inslow Works during May 1966.

A quick mention of the Standard in the shot, Riddles-designed engine 76102, built for BR at Doncaster Works, going into service in June 1957 and withdrawn from 67B Hurlford to be scrapped at Shipbuilding Industries, Faslane, in December 1966.

Black Five 4-6-0 No. 44888

A colourful view of Derby in 1964 as Black Five 44888 hauls a goods train along one of the many through lines. The Stanier-designed engine was built at Crewe Works during August 1945 and was withdrawn from 44C Lostock Hall. It made it to the end of main line steam on 31 August 1968 to be scrapped at Cashmore's of Great Bridge in May 1969.

EE Type 4 D255 Diesel

Type 4 Co-Co diesel enters Crewe station in 1962 with a group of interested trainspotters noting down the number. The engine was built at the English Electric Vulcan Foundry and introduced in January 1960. Its TOPS number later became 40055. It was withdrawn in November 1982 and scrapped at BREL Doncaster six months later.

Britannia Class 7, 4-6-2 No. 70028 *Royal Star*

Minus nameplates, *Royal Star* heads south over the
Mersey Bridge at the '12 Arches' near Warrington in 1966.
The locomotive was built at Crewe Works, going into
service on 27 October 1952. It was withdrawn from 12A
Carlisle Kingmoor in September 1966 and scrapped at
J. McWilliams of Shettleston four months later.

**Peak Class diesel No. D123 and Jubilee class 4-6-0
No. 45684 *Jutland***

A visit to Derby in February 1964 where a Peak Class diesel
D123 stands at the platform. This engine was built in Crewe
Works and delivered in October 1961. Its TOPS number was
45125. It was withdrawn in May 1987 and scrapped at BR
Eggington Junction soon after. *Jutland* was built at Crewe
Works in February 1936 and withdrawn from 27A Bank Hall
on 11 December 1965, being scrapped at Cashmore's of
Great Bridge three months later.

4-6-2 No. 4472 *Flying Scotsman'*
The history of *Flying Scotsman* is well documented, but
here is a photo of it in Trafford Park MPD. The engine has
been prepared for its run on the 'High Peak Railtour' with
the LCGB on 18 September 1965.

MSC Tank 0-6-0 No. 64 with the 'Pay Coach'
Another interesting industrial locomotive in the form of
a 'Long' tank Hudswell Clark locomotive built for the
Manchester Ship Canal Co. (MSC). It is seen attached to
the engineer's coach, which is acting as the pay coach for
its employees along the length of the canal. It is seen here
at Latchford Locks in 1962. The MSC railway was not
nationalised and became the largest private railway system
in Britain. It was built to service the company's docks. At its
peak it employed some 800 employees, with seventy-five
locomotives, over 2,000 wagons and 200 miles of track.
The line was closed to all traffic in 1978.

Warship Class D838 _Rapid_

It's 1963 and at Hereford we see a mixture of steam and diesel as D838
Rapid leaves with a long passenger train. _Rapid_ was built be the North British
Locomotive Works in Glasgow and entered service in September 1960. It was
withdrawn in March 1971 and cut up at BREL Swindon in March 1972.

Hughes Fowler Crab 2-6-0 No. 42817 and new Sulzer BO-BO type 2 No. D5137
In the shed at Longsight MPD in Manchester during 1961 and we see a Hughes Fowler Crab and a newly delivered Type 2 Bo-Bo Class 24 Diesel. The Crab was built at Horwich Works in July 1929, withdrawn from 9B Stockport Edgeley in April 1965 and scrapped at the Central Wagon Company, Ince, Wigan six months later. The diesel was built at BR Derby during October 1960, received the TOPS number 24137, and was withdrawn in July 1976 then scrapped at BREL Doncaster in October 1978.

Saddle Tank 0-4-0T No. 47005

Seen on the scrap line at Canklow in 1966, No. 47005 will shortly be delivered to Arnott Young at Parkgate for cutting up. It was built in Horwich Works during October 1953 and withdrawn from 40E Langwith Junction in December 1966.

WD 2-8-0 No. 90170

One of 935 locomotives designed by Riddles, built for the Ministry of Supply and bought by British Rail. No. 90170 heads north of Warrington at Winwick Junction in 1962. The engine was built be the North British Locomotive Works (Hyde Park) in 1943. It was withdrawn from 26B Agecroft in July 1963 and scrapped at W.E. Smiths of Ecclesfield during February 1965.

A1 Pacific 4-6-2 No. 60119 *Patrick Stirling*
At Doncaster MPD in May 1963 for a close-up of an A1 Pacific that was
built at Doncaster Works in 1948. It was withdrawn from 36A Doncaster
on 31 May 1964 and scrapped at Cox & Danks of Wadsley Bridge during
August 1965. It embarrassed itself somewhat one Christmas Eve when it
derailed whilst backing on to the *Queen of Scots* at Kings Cross. It was
named after Patrick Stirling, the GNR Superintendent from 1866 to 1895.

Castle Class 4-6-0 No. 5014 *Goodrich Castle*
No. 5014 heads south on a Cardiff–Manchester passenger train near
Hereford in May 1963. Built for the GWR at Swindon Works in June 1932,
its last shed was 84E Tyseley from where it was withdrawn in February 1965
and scrapped at Cashmore's of Great Bridge three months later.

Britannia Class 4-6-2 No. 70013 *Oliver Cromwell*
It is the lead up to that day in August when regular steam traction would
end, but in this month of August there were many rail tours to be had.
In preparation for this, one engine was serviced, painted and touched up
prior to the very last days and here it is seen on shed. More to come on
Oliver Cromwell later.

Two Black Fives Nos 45330 and 44890

Not all locomotives can haul specials during this last week of steam on British Rail in August 1968. Here two Black Fives wait patiently at Manchester Victoria for their next banking duty on Miles Platting Bank. 45330 was built at Armstrong Whitworth during March 1937 and withdrawn from 11A Carnforth on 31 August 1968 to be scrapped at Cohens, Cargo Fleet in December. No. 44890 was built at Crewe Works in 1945, withdrawn at the end of August from 26A Newton Heath and scrapped at Neptune Street Goods Yard, Hull, in November 1968.The end of regular steam traction on the main line came on 3 August 1968. British Rail were engaged in many meetings to discuss the continued use of steam on the main line, if only for enthusiast specials using privately owned traction. These optimistic murmurings, however, were to come to nothing, the BRB had a regime change at their headquarters at 222 Marylebone Road, London, and they were just as emphatic as the previous administration. It was decided to look to the future, not the past, and steam was the past. Privately owned steam traction would not be allowed on the main line anymore. There was one exception, however – Alan Pegler had an agreement with British Rail that *Flying Scotsman* had a contract to use selected routes until 1971. Other than that, a special order had been given to allow privately owned steam locomotives on the main line during 1968 but only until the end of mainline steam. This rule left many privately owned locomotives, some recently overhauled, restricted to the then few private lines over short distances. This rule did not slow the burgeoning of new and existing private lines and fortunately this would not be in vain and would prove massively popular.

Patricroft Railway Station, August 1967

The line from Liverpool to Manchester was opened in 1830, going from Liverpool Crown Street to Liverpool Road in Manchester. However, soon after opening, Liverpool Road was closed to passengers in 1844 and operated freight only. This station is now incorporated into the Manchester Museum of Science and Industry. The original first station on the line was Edge Hill, the oldest station still operating, and that was moved when the tunnels were completed from Lime Street. The work on Liverpool Lime Street and the tunnels to Edge Hill was commenced in 1832 and opened on 15 October 1836, taking over from Crown Street, which also became a goods station only. One of the stations on the line was Patricroft, which was situated on the world's first inter-city railway and next to what was the first commercial canal.

In this photo, we see the station and Patricroft Motive Power Depot 19C, which is behind the footbridge from which the photo was taken. Now there is just the station with shelters on each platform, but in 1967 it was a busy scene, with an unknown 8F locomotive and its train of ballast supplying the men working on the line. Plainclothes, pickaxes and shovels make up their dress and tools, as high viz jackets have not arrived yet, but the photo certainly gives us an insight into what it was like working on the permanent way in the days of steam.

5MT 4-6-0 No. 44916

Seen here at Newton Heath MPD in March 1967 is one of the ubiquitous Black Five locomotives, Stanier-designed and built at Crewe Works during December 1945 for the LMS. When Nationalisation arrived, the locomotive was allocated to 4A Bletchley. It was withdrawn from service at 9B Stockport Edgeley on 31 December 1967 and cut up at Drapers, Neptune Street Goods Yard, on 29 February 1968. A replica of this engine exists as a Hornby OO Gauge model.

8F 2-8-0 No. 48393

It's August 1967, and seen near Wrexham in charge of a coal train is 8F 2-8-0 No. 48393. The locomotive was built at Horwich Works and entered service in April 1945, later allocated to 16A Nottingham after Nationalisation. Remaining in service until the last day of revenue-earning steam traction, it was withdrawn from 10F Rose Grove on 3 August 1968 and condemned to be scrapped on the 8th.

We have reached the last day of regular steam working on British Rail, 3 August 1968. Steam could be seen on this last day at Preston station: the penultimate train was the 8.50 p.m. to Blackpool South, hauled by Black Five 45212. The platforms were packed and included two men suitably dressed in black attire and with long beards ceremoniously carrying a mock coffin along the platform, mourning the end of steam on British Rail. When you look at photos of the engines involved in these very last days of steam, note that they look a lot cleaner than others. This is mainly down to the groups of enthusiasts who spent the last few weeks cleaning and polishing them, sometimes with permission but other times covertly, but what they did provided the last days of steam with respectable-looking locomotives. Enthusiasts had arrived in the North West from all over the country. In groups, they cleaned and polished the engines that were to be used, even painting the buffer bars and buffers, making names and numbers to replace those missing, and generally making them look respectable. Steam working on the Western Region finished at the end of 1965. In Scotland and on the Southern Region it was no more after 1967. This left just the North West to last until 1968, hence the influx of enthusiasts. The strict Health and Safety rules had not yet arrived and films of the last days show massed ranks of enthusiasts all over the rails, bridges and embankments. Those last few days were unforgettable for those present!

Black Five 4-6-0 45212
The engine hauling the penultimate ordinary service steam working was Black Five 45212, with driver Bob Barker and fireman Mel Rigby. It was built at Armstrong Whitworth during November 1935 and withdrawn on 31 August 1968 from Lostock Hall. Its celebrated duty was not to be forgotten as it was preserved and now looks beautiful on the Keighley and Worth Valley Railway.

The 9.25 p.m. Glasgow train from Preston to Liverpool Exchange was to be the last ordinary rostered steam working on British Rail and the engine on that train was Black Five 4-6-0 45318, hauling the train from Preston to the now defunct Liverpool Exchange and driven by driver Ernie Hayes and fireman Tony Smith. The Stanier engine was built at Armstrong Whitworth in February 1937. Despite being the very last steam engine to haul a regular working on British Rail, it was not to be saved and was withdrawn from 24C Lostock Hall on 31 August 1968 and scrapped at Neptune Street Goods Yard of Hull during March 1969.

Two Black Fives Nos 45017 and 44874
Here are a group of enthusiasts with cameras and books around double-headed Black Five 45017 as it sets off from Manchester Victoria on Sunday, 4 August 1968 with 1Z79 as above. The engine was built at Crewe Works during May 1935 and its last shed was 11A Carnforth, from where it was withdrawn during August 1968 and scrapped at Drapers Neptune Street Goods Yard, Hull, on 30 April 1969. The lead engine 4-6-0 44874 was built at Crewe Works in April 1945. Its last shed was 11A Carnforth and it was withdrawn during August 1968 and scrapped at Drapers Neptune Street Goods Yard, Hull, on 31 March 1969.

Black Five 4-6-0s 45017 and 44874 double-head

There were fifteen specials on the day after 3 August culminating with the Fifteen Guinea Special on 11 August. Here are a few of the specials that ran on 4 August, the last official day of steam, until British Rail's Fifteen Guinea Special on 11 August. Here on Sunday, 4 August 1968, is one of them.

A Stephenson Locomotive Society special (1Z79) 'Farewell to Steam Rail Tour' from Manchester Victoria to Huddersfield that returned via Copy Pit. The tour itself started and finished at Birmingham New Street but these engines covered the length that was powered by steam traction.

Britannia Class 4-6-2 No. 70013 *Oliver Cromwell* **and 5MT 4-6-0 No. 44781**
The two engines are seen near Blackburn on 4 August 1968 hauling Stage 1
of the 'End of Steam Locomotive Club of Great Britain Farewell to Steam Rail
Tour' (reporting number 1Z74) that had started in London St Pancras. *Oliver
Cromwell* and Black Five 44781 were to take the train from Manchester
Victoria to Blackburn.

Two Black Fives Nos 45390 and 45025

Having taken over the 1Z74 Stage 3 of the LCGB Steam Special from Carnforth to Hellifield, Blackburn and Farrington Street is seen near Blackburn, on 4 August 1968. No. 45390 was built at Armstrong Whitworth in August 1937 and withdrawn from 11A Carnforth on 30 August 1963, then scrapped at Drapers, Neptune Street Goods Yard, Hull, two months later. No. 45025 was built at the Vulcan Foundry and withdrawn on 31 of August from Carnforth but was preserved and can be found on the Strathspey Railway in Scotland where, at the time of writing, it is undergoing a major refit.

Two Black Fives Nos 44871 and 44894
It is 4 August 1968 and Nos 44871 and 44894 are on 1Z78, near Blackburn with the Manchester Victoria to Stockport leg of the Stephenson Locomotive Society (Midland Area) 'Farewell to Steam Railtour No. 1', the tour that started in Birmingham. No. 44894 was built at Crewe Works in September 1945. It was withdrawn from 11A Carnforth on 31 August 1968 and scrapped in May 1969 at Drapers, Neptune Street Goods Yard, Hull. More on No. 44871 later.

8F 2-8-0 No. 48476 and Standard 5MT 4-6-0 No. 73069
Still 4 August 1968 and these three coupled engines await their tour of duty
on 1L50, organised by the Railway Correspondence and Travel Society as
the 'End of Steam Commemorative Rail Tour'. For the patient enthusiasts
there were many hiccups, such as the 8F being in quite a poor condition and
having to be taken off the train at Blackburn; it was said that the Standard
had to pull the train and push the 8F for a lot of the way! It was replaced
with a truly scruffy Black Five, No. 45407, but all was forgiven and despite
this an enjoyable time was had by all. The 8F was built at Swindon Works
between 1943 to 1945 it was withdrawn and scrapped later in the year. The
Standard 5MT 73069 was built in November 1954 at Crewe Works and its
last shed was Carnforth, from where it was withdrawn on 31 August 1968
and scrapped at Cashmore's of Newport in March 1969.

Britannia Class 70013 *Oliver Cromwell*
This locomotive Is seen on Stage 3 of the RCTS 'End of Steam Commemorative Tour' 1L50 on 4 August 1968. The driver was Brian McFadden and the route was from Lostock to Southport and Olive Mount, but there was a diversion due to delays.

5MT 4-6-0 No. 44874
Seen on another one of the end of steam specials is 5MT 44874 in Manchester Victoria. Enthusiasts share a platform with the soon-to-be-redundant equipment for steam traction. Note the typical dress of the boys for the period: shorts and bags – a closer look would reveal Ian Allen Locospotter books and an assortment of pens.

14 THE FIFTEEN GUINEA SPECIAL 1T57

The Fifteen Guinea Special was the last train to run on British Rail metals before a ban was imposed, starting on 12 August 1968. Fifteen pounds and fifteen shillings was an expensive treat for the enthusiasts who could afford it. The special ran from Liverpool Lime Street, setting off at 9.10 a.m., to Carlisle via Manchester Victoria and was hauled from Liverpool to Manchester by Black Five 45110. *Oliver Cromwell* took over the train from Manchester to Carlisle and then for the return two double-headed Black Fives took over for the trip back to Manchester. They were Nos 44781 and 44871, the latter was preserved and is at the East Lancashire Railway. No. 44781 was not so lucky: it was derailed for the film *The Virgin Soldiers* and scrapped on site by Kings of Norwich.

Britannia Class 4-6-2 No. 70013 Standard Class *Oliver Cromwell*

This is the most important of the engines that worked the last month of main line steam. Unlike the Black Fives and Standard that also worked the last of the specials on that fateful 11 August 1968, *Oliver Cromwell* and two of its three Black Five partners were not thanked by being summarily scrapped. The Ivatt-designed locomotive was built at Crewe Works in May 1951 and allocated to 32A Norwich Thorpe; its last shed was 11A Carnforth. It was officially withdrawn from BR on 17 of August 1968. Black Five 45110 took over at Manchester Victoria and hauled the train back to Liverpool. That was thought at the time to be the last ever steam working on British Railways, apart from the *Vale of Rheidol* (until it was privatised) and *The Flying Scotsman*.

Black Five 45110
Seen at Lostock Hall, Preston, on the last day of steam. This rather melancholy shot shows the driver perhaps contemplating his future in a steam-free British Rail.

Opposite: **Black Five 45110**
Now back in the shed at Lostock Hall after the last BR steam working. Black Five 45110 was preserved and can now be found on the Severn Valley Railway named *RAF Biggin Hill*. The 8F in front of it, No. 48294, was built by Beyer Peacock in 1941 for the WD and later bought by BR. It was withdrawn on 3 August from this shed and cut up in February 1969.

It was intended that on withdrawal Oliver Cromwell would become part of the National Railway Museum list and, accordingly, it was given permission to return to its old shed at Norwich on 12 August and then the following day to Diss under its own steam to go into preservation. It was taken the short distance from there by road to Bressingham Steam Museum and Gardens on loan, where it was engaged giving footplate rides until 2004. It was then decided to restore it for return to the main line in time for the fortieth anniversary of the end of steam in 2008. Its first trip out on completion of the restoration was a rerun of the Fifteen Guinea Special on 10 August 2008. The locomotive is still owned by the National Railway Museum.

FINALE

As we reach the end of this look at the final weeks of steam on British railways, we look back at what we had and what has now become extremely popular. The early 1970s saw steam return to selected routes on closed lines and the birth of the preservation groups. Soon, it would be allowed back onto the main lines, and classic trains can now be seen with steam traction once again.

The foresight of British Railways left a lot to be desired when they ruthlessly ordered the scrapping of perfectly good steam engines. But now things have changed, and the hypnotic smell of smoke, steam and oil can once again be enjoyed by an ageing group of baby boomers who remember the good old days, and a younger group of new enthusiasts can discover it. These new enthusiasts can use this book as a window into a time when steam ruled the metals and when drivers started their career as engine cleaners and slowly worked their way up the ladder to become top link drivers. Now trips on steam-hauled trains can be enjoyed by all. We hope you enjoyed a peep into those long-gone days when steam ruled the rails.

NEW STEAM LOCOMOTIVES

In August 1968 there was much sadness when people believed that steam on the railways of Britain had gone for good. Now, thanks to the hard work and dedication of the full-time and voluntary staff of the preserved railways, it has not. Below is a list of just some of the steam traction that is and will be gracing the metals. They will be joining the preserved steam locomotives already there that have been rescued from the cutter's torch and lovingly restored.

The sadness of 1968 has turned to joy as enthusiasts old and new have many opportunities to enjoy all that steam trains have to offer. The main BR workshops have now either closed or been turned over to other uses such as shopping centres and the like, with the exception of Crewe, which still has a facility for the repair of locomotives and the manufacture of parts on a smaller scale. However, across the country, there are preserved railways, most with their own workshops, where the maintenance of locomotives and the building of new ones is in full swing.

New steam locomotives that are completed or under construction:

At the Llangollen workshops: The Betton Grange Society (6880 *Betton Grange*), The Great Western Society (4709 *Night Owl*), The LMS Patriot Project (5551 *The Unknown Warrior* & 2-6-4T 42424), B17 Steam Locomotive Trust (61673 *Spirit of Sandringham*)

The Didcot Railway Centre: 1014 The G.W County Project (*GWR 1014 County of Glamorgan*), The Great Western Society (2999 *Lady of Legend*), Steam Railmotor Project (*GWR Steam Railmotor*)

Tyseley Locomotive Works: LNWR Bloomer Project (670 *Bloomer Class*), The Holden F5 Locomotive Trust (789 *GER Class*)

South Yorkshire Aircraft Museum Doncaster: P2 Steam Locomotive Company (*LNER 2001 Cock o' the North*)

Darlington Locomotive Works: The A1 Steam Locomotive Trust (*LNER 60163 Tornado*), The P2 Steam Locomotive Company (*2007 Prince of Wales*) The A1 Steam Locomotive Trust (*LNER V4 Bantam Cock* and *LNER V3*)

Mizens Railway: Engine 61662 Appeal (restoration of 61662 *Manchester United*)

Whitwell and Reepham Railway: Claud Hamilton Locomotive Group (8783 *Phoenix*)

Hackworth Industrial Park, Shildon: G5 Locomotive Company (*LNER Class* 1759)

Great Central Railway, Nottingham: GCR 567 Locomotive Group (*LNER Class* 567)

Bluebell Railway: Reconstruction of (32424 *Beachy Head, Standard 2MT* 84030)

Severn Valley Railway: 82045 Steam Locomotive Trust (3MT 82045)

West Somerset Railway: (*Mogul 9351*) LNWR George the Fifth Steam Locomotive Trust (*LMS 2013 Prince George*), General Steam Navigation Locomotive Restoration Society (35011 *General Steam Navigation*), Standard Steam Locomotive Company Ltd 'The Clan Project' (72010 *Hengist*), The Locomotive Group (3MT 77021)